LEADERSHIP IS A MARATHON

A Leadership Fable

JOYCE KADUKI

WestBow
PRESS®
A DIVISION OF THOMAS NELSON
& ZONDERVAN

Copyright © 2016 Joyce Kaduki.

All rights reserved. No part of this book may be used or reproduced by any means, graphic, electronic, or mechanical, including photocopying, recording, taping or by any information storage retrieval system without the written permission of the author except in the case of brief quotations embodied in critical articles and reviews.

WestBow Press books may be ordered through booksellers or by contacting:

WestBow Press
A Division of Thomas Nelson & Zondervan
1663 Liberty Drive
Bloomington, IN 47403
www.westbowpress.com
1 (866) 928-1240

Because of the dynamic nature of the Internet, any web addresses or links contained in this book may have changed since publication and may no longer be valid. The views expressed in this work are solely those of the author and do not necessarily reflect the views of the publisher, and the publisher hereby disclaims any responsibility for them.

Any people depicted in stock imagery provided by Thinkstock are models, and such images are being used for illustrative purposes only. Certain stock imagery © Thinkstock.

ISBN: 978-1-5127-3996-1 (sc)
ISBN: 978-1-5127-3998-5 (hc)
ISBN: 978-1-5127-3997-8 (e)

Library of Congress Control Number: 2016906803

Print information available on the last page.

WestBow Press rev. date: 05/10/2016

CONTENTS

Dedication vii

Acknowledgments ix

Introduction xi

1. Moment of Truth 1
2. Where Do We Go From Here? 19
3. The Search 30
4. Balance 52
5. Second Exit 66
6. Parallel Learning Path 78
7. Mentoring Moments 90
8. New Chapter? 105
9. Yearning for More 124
10. New Culture 142

Conclusion 149

Notes 151

DEDICATION

This book is dedicated to my teachers, mentors and coaches; and all those I have been privileged to mentor, coach and teach.

ACKNOWLEDGMENTS

I thank my husband, Ken Kaduki, whose love, friendship, support, encouragement, informal coaching and mentoring, constructive criticism when I needed it, and review of my writing has meant a great deal to me.

I also thank my son and daughter, Ndeda and Waigumo, who have been valuable reverse mentors and coaches to me. They have asked questions, challenged my assumptions and actions, and offered insights that have helped me look at life through their lenses. They have been instrumental in enabling me to develop a different, broader and richer worldview. In addition, my son Ndeda designed the front cover of this book. I am proud of his rising to the challenge.

A special thank you to my parents, Mr. Fredrick Njogu and Mrs. Bilha Waigumo, and to my parents-in-law, Mr. Elisha Kaduki and Mrs. Julia Njeri, for their prayers, nurture and counsel at various points of my life. They have taught me much.

I give my sincere gratitude to my brothers and sisters for being there for me and from whom I have learned much as we journey through life together. Their friendship and support have been invaluable.

I offer special thanks to my writing partner and friend, who is also a coach, Colleta Macharia, and to our family friend who is also a pastoral coach, Tim Ryder. Their insightful comments and very helpful suggestions on the content of this book cannot be overstated. As a result, the volume you hold in your hands is quite different from what I started off with.

I am grateful to Kari Mutu who edited the manuscript, thus providing valuable support in polishing it up.

Many other friends and colleagues in the people development profession have helped in vital ways, including peer accountability, support, encouragement, and challenging me to write this book.

The WestBow Press team has provided continuous support in the development of this book, and their accountability checks kept me writing even during those moments I second-guessed myself. They have also been instrumental in making this book available to the readers.

Finally, and foremost, I thank God for giving me the presence of mind, strength and all the resources I needed to write this book. He has made it possible.

INTRODUCTION

> "If you can't fly then run, if you can't run then walk, if you can't walk then crawl, but whatever you do you have to keep moving forward."
> Martin Luther King, Jr.

On February 15, 2015, Kenyan marathoner Hyvon Ng'etich was poised to win the Austin Marathon in the United States of America.

Ng'etich, 29, who was leading the women runners for most of the race, started losing steam and her body began giving up on her with about two kilometers remaining in the race.

She, however, continued running while stumbling and seemingly weak.

With the finish line in sight, Ng'etich was clearly overwhelmed and came crashing down on the tarmac in downtown Austin, a city about 320 kilometers south of Dallas.

Ng'etich was determined not to quit the race even as she was on her knees and in obvious pain. After a brief pause while on her hands and knees and with her forehead on the ground, she started an agonizing crawl toward the finish line.

The crowd gasped while some shed tears upon seeing her determination to finish the race in her condition. They cheered her on as she made several stops to catch her breath crawling slowly.

A nurse kept a close watch on Ng'etich as she continued crawling but made sure that a wheel chair was close in case she could not continue any longer. Both the nurse and the marathon officials refrained from helping her out, which would have led to her disqualification.

Ng'etich eventually crossed the finish line, still on her hands and knees.

She could excusably have given up along the way, especially after her body gave way. But she did not. Determined to finish the race even when she was visibly battered, she pushed herself to cross the finish line.

Ng'etich's perseverance is a sterling example of what it sometimes takes to complete a marathon. A marathon is an endurance race. On some stretches you are in good form and do just fine. You make good time. You enjoy the race. But there are also some moments where the going gets tough. Your body becomes weary and threatens to give way. Whatever the circumstances, as Ng'etich did, you need to keep your eyes on the finish line and avoid distractions. If you stick it out and keep moving forward even when your progress is painstakingly slow, you will eventually get to the finish.

Leadership is a lot like running a marathon. It is long, tough, and characterized by inter-changing moments of encouragement and heartbreak. Leadership can wear down even the strongest athlete.

For a leader, as for a marathoner, the journey is marked by both high and low moments, the good and the bad, gains and pains. Sometimes you get results that are very different from what you expected. You face triumphs, but also disappointments and discouragements. It's not always easy to lead and keep growing and developing. Like Ng'etich who was winning in some stretches but also had to crawl when the going got really tough, you'll find the same is true of your leadership experience. Let the wins and the easy stretches spur you on. When the temptation to quit is at its strongest, keep your eyes on the finish line and keep moving forward until you cross it. Choice by choice, decision by decision, action by action, determine to keep moving even when your body—and even the people around you—tell you that it's time to quit. After all, it's a marathon not a sprint that you win with a single short dash.

When the weight of leading takes its toll and you slow down to a crawl, you might get tempted to give up. Don't! Heed Martin Luther King Jr's advice that, "If you can't fly then run, if you can't run then walk, if you can't walk then crawl, but whatever you do you have to keep moving forward."

This book uses a fable to drive this message home. It's an astonishingly simple fable and that is intentional. This is because the author's main purpose is not to entertain, in which case the reader would have been presented with a complex and enthralling work of fiction.

Rather, the book is aimed at driving home some fundamental principles of leadership in a context that makes the lessons stick. Of particular note is the role that mentoring and coaching play in the development of leaders. Younger and less experienced employees and leaders can learn from more seasoned leaders, learning from both their failures and successes. Younger leaders can teach older leaders, too. And even experienced leaders and teams can learn a great deal and become even better from working with other members of their teams, and with coaches.

Above all, one has to remain persistent and determined so as to grow and be effective as a leader.

CHAPTER 1

MOMENT OF TRUTH

Pay attention to the whispers, so you won't have to listen to the screams.
Cherokee Proverb

The First Exit

The moment Mark Zito returned to the boardroom of Precision Tools and Instruments Industries (PTI Industries), he could tell something was wrong. Very wrong. He took his time getting back to his seat, as he quickly took the scene in.

The non-executive board chair, Madam Patricia Shilingi–Madam P as she was popularly known–was speaking animatedly on her cellphone. She quickly wrapped up her conversation. Jeff, a lawyer who ran his own law practice, sat pensively with his arms folded across his chest. Chris, the most vocal member of the board, was quiet, which was unusual. He always had something to say. Marilyn, the newest member on the board, seemed to be in a heated discussion with two other members, Eileen and Patrick. At the far end of the room stood Nancy and James in yet another private conversation. Leon was absent, having given apologies earlier as he was traveling.

As Mark took his seat, everyone settled down quickly and almost on cue, turned to look at him. He had been requested to leave the board members to caucus after an uneasy discussion on the company's performance. Results for the previous year were dismal and he had been hard-pressed to explain why. Despite his attempts to justify the outcome, a majority of the board members had concluded that the performance was unacceptable.

Mark tried to occupy his mind by looking at the reports in front of him. He waited. Except for the humdrum noise of the air conditioner, the room was quiet. After a few moments of awkward silence, Madam P looked directly at Mark and said with a note of finality, "On behalf of the entire board, I want to let you know that we have made the difficult decision to let you go. It was as hard for us to arrive at this decision as we imagine it will likely be difficult for you to come to terms with. We have had a good working relationship with you and we had envisioned working together for a long time to come. However, there are several parameters we can't ignore."

She paused, as if waiting for her words to sink in. "Although the market for Precision Tools has grown steadily over the last five years, since you became chief executive officer three years ago, our market share has shrunk by at least 20 percent. In addition, profit margins have gone down, staff morale has plummeted, and turnover is at its highest."

The news hit Mark like a punch in the belly. He felt dizzy as he fleetingly looked first at Madam P, then at each of the board members seated around the oval-shaped mahogany table. Its finely polished surface that had looked elegant only moments before, now appeared cold. He shuddered as a feeling of isolation swept over him. He wished he could step outside, if only for a moment, to escape the penetrating looks of those who were now openly staring at him. But leaving the room was not an option. It would be awkward, to say the least. In any case, he felt paralyzed and glued to his seat. Even if he attempted to leave, he wasn't sure his legs could take him past the boardroom door without buckling under him. There was no use in trying. So he just sat there and steadied himself by gripping the armrests of his executive chair. On the surface he looked calm and only slightly fluttered. Underneath however, it was as if he was being tossed over and over by huge tsunami waves that he was absolutely powerless against.

She's so casual, you'd think she was announcing that the price of bread had gone up marginally, thought Mark.

Being the quintessential diplomat, Madam P was the picture of composure. She looked around the room before continuing in a somewhat conciliatory tone. "Even though you have been doing your best, as you have continually assured us, your efforts are not bearing the sort of results we've been looking for." She glanced away momentarily and then said, "In light of your dedicated service at PTI Industries over the last eight years, we are giving you the option to give notice. Your departure will therefore be announced as a resignation.

"We will allow a three-month transition period during which time we will recruit a new CEO. We expect you to work alongside the new hire before you leave." She paused, as if waiting for the message to sink in in its entirety, and then asked, "Do you have any comments or questions?"

In just a few sentences, Madam P had delivered what sounded like a life sentence. Mark could never, in his worst nightmare, have imagined that his time at PTI Industries would come to an end in the manner unfolding before his eyes. While his time at the company had not been perfect, he had largely enjoyed himself. He had always imagined himself remaining an employee there for a while, possibly another ten years or so, and then retiring voluntarily.

That was not to be. He didn't trust himself to speak without betraying the emotions he was battling with. He slowly took a sip of water and then a deep breath. He raked his mind for a politically correct statement. *How do you respond to the news that your employer no longer needs your services?* He wondered.

After what seemed like an eternity but was really just a minute, he managed to say as calmly as he possibly could, "I appreciate your giving me the news in person, instead of through the telephone or a press release." The board members laughed lightly. He reasoned he'd lost everything, that there was nothing else to lose, so he might as well be candid. "Well, the news has taken me by surprise. I need time to let it sink in. I will therefore reserve my comments for now." There were understanding nods all round.

Madam P said, "I'd like to have a meeting with you in three days' time, to agree on a transition plan."

"Fair enough," said Mark, grateful that he didn't have to say any more for now.

"We'll release you," Madam P said, "and the rest of us will take a few minutes to wrap up our discussions."

Mark wished the board members a good afternoon and walked out slowly, in a daze.

He was grateful there was no member of staff hanging around the corridor, as he was in no mood for small talk. He headed straight to his office. As he passed by his personal assistant's desk, he said, "Enid, I don't want any interruptions for the rest of the day. You can brief me on any matters needing my attention when we have our regular review tomorrow morning." That communicated to Enid Kaka that even she was not welcome.

Going into his office, he closed the door behind him and sat down heavily. Elbows on the table, he dropped his head into his open palms, closed his eyes, and just let thoughts rush through.

Regret

Mark hadn't seen it coming. True, the company had made only marginal profits that were just higher than the rate of inflation in the first year he was at the helm, and subsequently made losses two years in a row. *But this*? Once Mark's initial shock was over, he felt dejected. And then angry. Why hadn't anyone given him a warning? True, boards sacked CEOs without notice often enough, but *this* board? Not even an alert at a personal level? He had enjoyed a fairly cordial working relationship with most members of the board, and couldn't help but feel a sense of betrayal, especially when he considered that the company's dismal performance was not for lack of trying on his part. *But then, if I'm not responsible, who is?*

It didn't take Mark long to realize that no matter how much he agonized over the loss of his job, he couldn't turn back the clock. He could not possibly go back to the board and beg them to let him stay. It seemed a bit late in the day for that. In any case, his ego was too big for such an act.

Thinking about his career and planning his next move was unquestionably better use of his time. Three months would not be adequate for him to find another job at his level. And yet a glaring gap on his CV would not do him any good. Absolute retirement was out of the question. At fifty-one years of age, Mark still had the agile mind of a twenty-something year old and energy to boot.

His life's journey flashed through his mind. Born in a family of eight children, his father had been employed as an accountant at a local bank. He worked late nights and most weekends and was rarely at home. His mother taught at a high school located five kilometers from their home. In the evenings and over weekends, she worked on the family's one-acre piece of land which was adjacent to their house. The fruits and vegetables she grew supplemented the family's diet.

As the firstborn in the family, Mark started learning responsibility from an early age. Occasionally, his mother asked him to help in the garden. When he wasn't accompanying her, he was left in charge of his siblings, maintaining order during play and supervising their homework.

He moved to a boarding school when he got to high school but even then, he continued with his family chores during the holidays. By the time he completed high school he had already decided to pursue a business degree and follow in his father's footsteps.

Mark's career followed a more or less conventional path. After graduating from university with an accounting major, he landed his first job with a reputable audit firm. He immediately embarked on a professional accounting course, qualifying as a certified public accountant two and a half years later. He quickly rose through the ranks and finally exited the audit firm to join PTI Industries as a management accountant.

Mark rapidly earned the respect of his colleagues and bosses for his hard work and dedication, and was soon promoted to a finance manager position. With time, he was appointed chief finance officer. He held the latter position until his appointment as CEO three years ago.

While Mark had impeccable work ethics, he didn't seem particularly interested in building close relationships with co-workers, referring to it as the touchy-feely side of business which was too soft for his liking. If that was the only area he needed to grow in, he possibly could have gotten by, albeit with a bit of struggle. But Mark was not much of a visionary. He was content to maintain the status quo so long as business seemed to be running smoothly. Therefore, once he took over the reins at PTI Industries he let the company just grow organically. At board or management team meetings he often liked to say that, "If it's working, let it be. No need to rock the boat." He seemed oblivious to the fact that things had stopped working at PTI Industries for over two years now. His laissez-faire attitude had been a constant source of conflict between him and Madame P who took every opportunity to point out that the business had the potential to double in size in a few years. She was increasingly frustrated that she could not see that happening with Mark at the helm. In hindsight, Mark wished he had taken Madam P's remarks more seriously.

Strained Conversation

As Mark sat deep in thought, he recalled an odd conversation he had had with Jeremy Sani, head of production, barely eleven months before. Jeremy had invited him to lunch, over which they had mainly discussed general business issues. When they were taking dessert however, their conversation had taken a different turn. Jeremy had begged permission to be a little direct with him.

Sensing the hesitation on Jeremy's part, Mark had urged him on, "Fire away!"

Jeremy started haltingly, "I hope you'll take what I'm going to say in the spirit in which it is intended. I share it as feedback aimed at building up, not tearing down."

"You can be candid with me." Mark encouraged him, wondering what was coming.

"As you know, I have been an ardent student of leadership for quite a while," Jeremy started. Mark nodded. Jeremy was not only known for his extensive library of leadership books, journals, and CDs, but had also established for himself a reputation of being the go-to person on the executive team when people needed either unbiased feedback or a solid sounding board to bounce off ideas.

Jeremy continued, "It's a long story, but goes back to my first formal mentoring relationship early in my career. Peter Sage, who was more of a big brother than a boss to me, gave me my first real lessons in leadership. He kept referring to life as a marathon rather than a sprint. With time, I came to realize that leadership too, is like a marathon in many respects. I started jotting down analogies between leadership and running a marathon. I have quite a collection now. That process culminated in the birth of my leadership philosophy." Jeremy looked lost in his own world for a moment. "Sadly, Peter died from a heart attack ten years ago, but the seed he planted in me took root and bore fruit, and continues to be expressed through my leadership."

Early Lesson

"One of many early lessons was about care and comradeship. Serious marathoners don't go to the race alone. Often, they practice with others, exchange notes, and cheer one another on. Similarly, the leadership journey calls for development of mutual trust and friendship with others who have a similar aim. When it comes to followers, this is expressed by reaching out to them and letting them know that you sincerely care."

Mark listened keenly as Jeremy continued, "When you take the time to connect with people, support them, and cheer them on, you often get better results. I've applied this principle in my work over the years and I'm amazed by the positive results I get with my peers and colleagues every time. Caring has enabled me to promote the growth of healthy working relationships among the production team members. It has also made it easier for me to demand higher levels of performance from people, as they know first and foremost that I'm genuinely concerned about them. We've seen their ability to develop new concepts soar and they have been bursting with ideas. I believe it is something that can be rolled out to the rest of the company," Jeremy concluded.

"I can't argue with that. The results from your unit remain consistently positive," said Mark, secretly wondering whether Jeremy was preparing the ground to ask for a salary increase.

Rocking The Boat

"I don't mean to undermine you, but just wish to share my honest opinion" Jeremy resumed. "I feel that relationship-building is an area where our company has lots of room for improvement. When I talk with my team members, many of them indicate that while they are doing their best to make positive contributions in their individual roles, outside of the production team they feel neither cared for nor recognized as people. To put it bluntly, they might as well be fixed assets. A number of staff in other departments make reference to the same, and talk about feeling disconnected from one another. In different conversations I've had, several employees say they don't feel as professionally challenged as they wish they were, which they attribute to things not seeming to change much around here. Many seem to have no sense of direction. Last week, I had a conversation with our chief information officer, Jake Bima, and heard similar sentiments. In the spirit of care and candor, I felt the need to bring this to your attention."

Jeremy waited for any reactions from Mark. Receiving none, he said, "I would be happy to support you in finding out the real issues keeping our company's performance down, and to help address them so as to improve results." Jeremy looked directly at Mark, and signaled he was done.

Mark looked back at Jeremy and said with the slightest hint of defensiveness and sarcasm, "When you lead just one department, generating good results is easy. There are not too many external factors to upset your performance. That also leaves you with plenty of time to bond with your team. Leading a whole company is very complicated, but I don't suppose you understand just how much. I believe we'll get further as an organization if we respect one another's space and efforts."

He paused briefly and then continued, a tad coldly, "You seem to be spending a lot of time on people issues. Have you spoken to Shirley on the same?" Jeremy knew that Mark was referring to Shirley Asali, head of human resources. Secretly, he was convinced that this was a matter requiring action at the topmost leadership level but given Mark's cold-hearted response, he decided not to push the matter. He had said enough for one day, and could always pick up on the conversation at a later date. This was not to be, however, as a rift had slowly started developing between them after that conversation.

Mark had felt irritated at what he had perceived as presumptuous, judgmental, and overconfident behavior on Jeremy's part. He had tried hard not to show it, but he started looking for an opportunity to put Jeremy in his place.

Leading Up

On his part, Jeremy had been watching his boss and listening to his team and peers, and he was bothered that Mark seemed oblivious to the fact that the organization was going downhill. The situation seemed to be getting progressively worse. He had contemplated giving feedback to Mark several times in the past couple of months, but had chickened out each time.

He was torn between preserving cordial relations with his boss and upsetting him with what he considered as the unpleasant truth. Mark had a reputation of reacting explosively when provoked so there was no telling what might follow after that kind of feedback.

Finally realizing that he would not be doing his boss a favor by withholding the much-needed feedback, Jeremy had decided to bite the proverbial bullet and speak to Mark. After all, as his mentor often told him, leading one's boss means being bold enough to confront them with the truth even when it had the potential to blow up in your face. What mattered was that one approached the boss in a candid, respectful manner. There simply was no guarantee of the feedback being received well.

After agonizing over it for several weeks, Jeremy decided it would be easier to live with the consequences of being courageous enough to do what needed to be done, than not taking action and preserving his skin as things fell apart. That culminated in the lunch meeting which brought about a strain in their relationship.

Hindsight

Mark now wondered whether he shouldn't have been more accommodating of Jeremy. At the time, he thought Jeremy was just being critical and so he hadn't really taken heed. *I should have encouraged him to talk a little more*, he thought. Maybe Jeremy had meant well, and could possibly have helped to avert the crisis at hand. Perhaps Mark should even have taken Jeremy's offer of support?

Wasn't that what Mark's late Uncle Charlie used to say about leadership, that listening to whispers will help you avoid hearing the screams which follow those who did not pay attention? Madam P's regular expressions of dissatisfaction and the conversation with Jeremy were clearly the whispers which Mark had ignored at his own peril.

The more Mark thought about the whole saga, the more he realized that the writing had been on the wall for some time. He just hadn't seen it for what it was. Unfortunately, he couldn't turn back the clock now, his fate was sealed.

Mark's torrent of thoughts was finally interrupted by the buzz of his cellphone. He was in no mood for conversations and was going to ignore the ring. However, he fleetingly glanced at the screen and noticed his wife's name, Alison, flashing. He picked the call.

"Daddy, why didn't you come for my piano recital? You had promised you would because it was the last one this season." Zarina, his seventh-grade daughter was on the other end. There was no mistaking the disappointment and hurt in her voice.

In an instant he remembered that he should have left the office three hours before so as to be in school on time. In the wake of the afternoon's session with the board, it had completely slipped his mind.

"I'm sorry, sweetheart. An emergency came up for daddy, but I'll make it up to you. I'll be on my way shortly." He knew it was a tired excuse because he had used it too many times over the last three years.

Perhaps on the drive home he could figure out something to pacify Zarina. She was normally the source of much laughter in their home and during the rare moments when she was down, it dampened the whole family atmosphere. This latest upset was not going to help.

Mark got up slowly and moved to the large window of his corner office. It overlooked the busy Mombasa Road in Nairobi, Kenya, on a stretch between the Jomo Kenyatta International Airport and the central business district. As he reached out to close the blinds he realized he had been brooding for quite a while since the city was already brightly lit by street lights and night lights from the skyscrapers. On a good evening, he would have spent several minutes watching the blazing car lights as vehicles inched their way eastwards, away from the city center. It never ceased to amaze Mark how the city emptied itself of both human and motor traffic only for the process to repeat itself all over again twenty-four hours later.

Tonight, though, he was distracted and thought only about himself. The lights of the slow-moving traffic somehow did not hold the usual magic and as if by coincidence, the traffic seemed to have come to a standstill. Mark thought that this was eerily reflective of what his career had been reduced to in one short afternoon. A grinding halt! His heart was as though it was enveloped by a strange dark cloud. Surely it couldn't get any worse – or could it?

Joyce Kaduki

The key lessons I learned in this chapter

The action steps I will take as a result

CHAPTER 2

WHERE DO WE GO FROM HERE?

Do not go where the path may lead, go instead where there is no path and leave a trail.
Ralph Waldo Emerson

Madam P

Three days later, Madam P sat in the small conference room of PTI Industries. She was in good form and could easily have passed for someone in her mid-forties. Her younger sister was fond of teasing her that, "At sixty years old, you wear your age well. When I grow up, I want to be just like you, Pattie!"

Madam P was clearly one of the oldest members of the board. This was her thirteenth year on the board and the last four of those years she had also served as the chair. Her tenure had seen the company grow before seeming to peak and then plateau.

She was disconcerted by the recent decline and was determined not to go down in the company's history as the one under whose watch the company disintegrated.

Previously, Madam P had worked for a telecommunications corporation through most of her career. The company was a monopoly for several decades during which time service to customers was average and innovation was unheard of. Rapid technological advancements in the industry, including the advent of the mobile phone, had driven the giant out of business leaving many employees redundant. Before her position was affected, Madam P had opted for early retirement and invested the bulk of her final dues in a franchise of a mobile handset company. It had been well received by the market and so Madam P was successful by many standards.

That transition had taught Madam P valuable lessons about reading the market and making the necessary changes to stay ahead. Over the last several months she had increasingly sensed the need for PTI Industries to make some changes.

PTI Industries

Madam P had arrived an hour earlier than her scheduled meeting with Mark. She had deliberately carved out this time to allow herself space to reflect further on the company's past leadership transitions, current state and future direction.

Madam P mentally retraced the company's leadership since inception twenty years ago. Initially set up to manufacture precision tools and instruments, the company had enjoyed instant success. Working through a small network of wholesalers who bought in bulk and distributed to the retail market, and without any significant competition, the company had soared to become a market leader. The company's first CEO, Gary Melo was mature, fatherly and decisive, at times slightly overbearing but he was always a gentleman. When he took office at forty-five years old he already had a receding hairline which made him look older than he really was. From then on he had successfully led the company for ten years, during which time the business remained a market leader. Following injuries suffered in a near-fatal road accident, Gary was forced into early retirement and was succeeded by Sheila Taben who was PTI Industries' head of strategy at the time.

Madame P smiled slightly as she remembered how the no-nonsense, tough-talking Sheila rattled the first board meeting as the new in-charge. After she shared her dreams for the company, the board members thought that she was too quick in spelling out what sounded like lofty ideas. When one of them challenged her about the need to first study the company before making assumptions, she had respectfully but firmly shot back saying that she had been around long enough to know what she was talking about. It turned out she had been right.

Sheila had gone on to build upon Gary's initial successes during her first four years at the helm. In her fifth year, she led the company in a strategic shift to start direct distribution of their products on the retail market. The move had been necessitated by the company's desire to be closer to the end-users of their products. The objective of the shift was to increase the company's market share and revenue, in addition to positioning the company to get firsthand feedback on how their products were doing. The information was fed into the product development process.

Sheila also challenged the team to embrace new technology in production. Initially, she encountered some resistance, mainly from the marketing team who believed the move could lead to an increase in prices and result in reduced sales. It would be counter-productive, they had argued. Once Sheila's mind was made up, however, there was no turning back. She insisted that that was the direction the company was moving in, leaving it to the production team to figure out how to make it happen without adversely affecting end-user prices.

Intensive consultations between production, sales and marketing, and the finance units followed. The finance team was keen to use only internal financing and avoid any form of debt. The company had been on a steady growth plan, building healthy reserves in the process. These would be used to cushion the company in the initial months when production costs would erode profits. It had been anticipated that in about eight months, the company would break even. What surprised many was that it took an even shorter period than expected. In two months flat the company recouped initial losses and broke even within four months.

Buoyed by the euphoria of that success, productivity had doubled and profit margins had risen before the end of the year. PTI Industries seemed poised for unprecedented growth that would put it miles ahead of its closest competitors. Then Sheila resigned. She had been offered a regional job with a multinational company in the Middle East. She had later confided to Madame P that the lure of the challenges and potential for growth associated with an international posting in a foreign country were irresistible.

Sheila recommended that Dick Sevetti, who had succeeded her as head of strategy after her elevation to CEO six years before, succeed her as the next CEO. Dick's stint at the helm had been uneventful. While PTI Industries remained profitable, there had been no spectacular gains as had been witnessed during Sheila's tenure. Dick's term had come to an abrupt end two years later following his appointment to a senior role in the government.

That was when Mark came onto the scene. He had been with the company for ten years by then and had had a solid performance track record. He seemed a natural fit for the job so when Dick proposed that he take over, the board unreservedly ratified his appointment. Just three months into his role however, questions relating to his leadership style and ability began to emerge. The demands from the finance team he had been leading were nothing compared to his newly expanded role of providing direction to the company, overseeing operations, leading the executive team, and working with the board and other external stakeholders.

For a while, the board assumed that they needed to give Mark time to settle into his new role and then performance would pick up. That was not to be. By the end of another three months, the company's performance took a turn for the worse. The losing streak had only just begun. A board member was to later recall that Mark had casually mentioned a couple of times that he was struggling. He had taken it as a joke given Mark's easy manner.

Looking back, Madam P regretted that the board hadn't pulled the plug earlier and relieved Mark of his responsibilities. But that was now water under the bridge.

As she mulled over Mark's inability in light of the company's desire for growth, it was obvious now that the two had been mismatched. Mark's impeccable professional competence ranked way above his leadership ability. Had the former been average and the latter exceptional, he possibly could have gotten by. At the last meeting after the board informed Mark about his dismissal, it was agreed that the new CEO must be able to pursue a bold vision so as to help turn the company back onto the profitability path. Members had agreed that the new leader should be a visionary with strong people skills, as they were convinced that the human element was what would deliver results. Mark was glaringly deficient in both respects. The board was understandably cautious not to have another CEO mismatch.

The Plan

Madam P's thoughts were interrupted by a light tap on the door. She quickly glanced at her watch; it was exactly 8:59 am. Mark walked briskly into the room. He was always punctual to a fault, which Madam P greatly admired. She realized she would miss that.

After a brief exchange of pleasantries, the two got straight to the business of the day. They agreed that the announcement about Mark's impending departure would be sent out to the company's executive team immediately. This would pave way for the recruitment process. The board wanted to uphold the tradition of hiring successors from within, a custom in line with the company's succession planning which was aimed at promoting talent retention.

The search would only be opened up to external candidates if an internal candidate could not be found. Going by the outcome of the last hire, however, the board acknowledged that they needed to engage in a more rigorous screening process instead of merely relying on the recommendation of an outgoing CEO. In any case, the old practices couldn't work because the executive exiting the company now was leaving under a cloud.

The board had decided to engage the services of an executive search firm to carry out the recruitment. Working with a dedicated team would ensure a more objective and thorough vetting process.

All heads of departments would be given due consideration and interviewed if they made the shortlist. As the search got underway, the rest of the staff would be informed about Mark's planned departure.

It was envisioned that the process would be quick since all the candidates were internal and any conflicts in schedules could be resolved easily. Candidates would be advised to make the process a priority and avail themselves at short notice.

Next, Madam P and Mark turned their attention to drafting the announcement to be sent out to the executive team. They agreed on brevity, simply stating that Mark had resigned and would be leaving after three months to pursue personal interests. This was followed by a short paragraph stating that given the brief transition period, recruitment would commence immediately, and that internal candidates would be given preference. The message would be sent out from Mark's email address but under both their signatures.

The Announcement

The email caused quite a stir the following day when it was received by the executive team members. On one hand, his resignation didn't come as a total surprise given the undertones in the office. On the other hand, most people read in-between the lines and guessed that Mark had been forced to resign. In hushed tones around the water cooler and over extended coffee breaks, they expressed surprise that there had been no hint of a warning from the board, at least, not as far as they knew. What did that mean for the successor?

However, that did not entirely dampen internal interests. After all, it had been obvious to most others—apart from Mark, it seemed—that the continued slide in performance would have soon put the company out of business.

In fact, barely a day after the notice had been sent out, Bob Muro, head of sales and marketing, openly joked to a couple of his peers that he would be moving office vertically in three months' time. This was in veiled reference to the CEO position.

Secretly, Jeremy Sani, who was head of production, found himself warming up to the possibility of succeeding Mark.

Sure, he had harbored ambitions to grow in his career, but had hitherto assumed it would be another year or two before he was ready to move up. That dream now seemed within reach.

Would any of them make it to the corner office?

The key lessons I learned in this chapter

The action steps I will take as a result

CHAPTER 3

THE SEARCH

The art of life is a constant readjustment to our surroundings.
Kakuzo Okakaura

A week later, Michelle Tate, the executive director of Plax, an executive search firm, sat in her office considering notes she had taken during a series of meetings with representatives of PTI Industries' board. She set them alongside a copy of the company's strategy, the CEO profile and the last five years' performance reports for the seven heads of division that she would be considering for the position. She had also obtained the relevant CVs, a summary of each division's strategy and their reports to the board for the last five years.

Michelle knew that she would need to work round the clock to meet the deadline which was barely three weeks away. Having conducted similar searches over twelve years for some of the largest companies locally and in the region, 95 percent of her hires had turned out right. This, more than anything else, gave her confidence that she could deliver.

Over the next week, Michelle prioritized the PTI Industries' recruitment and delegated what she could to her associate, Larry. He headed their Mombasa office situated just over two hundred and seventy miles away. This freed her to comb through the pile of documents on the side table in her office. The exercise was the one part of the executive hiring process that she preferred to handle personally. While laborious, it gave her the opportunity to get well acquainted with the candidates early and assess their potential fit with the company. It was aimed at avoiding costly mistakes which she had seen happen in her second year in business, after which she had made the personal commitment to never allow it to happen again.

Michelle made summary notes for each of the candidates as she went along, noting their backgrounds, strengths, accomplishments, areas of growth, and specific things she would need to probe further when she met with them. Through email, phone, and teleconferences, she bounced ideas off Larry. She also held a couple of telephone conversations with Madam P to ensure she had covered every detail that the board considered important. In one such conversation, she asked, "How critical is it that the preferred candidate have several years of board experience?"

Madam P's response was precise, "If it's a choice between number of years and level of engagement, the latter wins hands down."

Michelle was thankful that following each conversation and from reviewing the documents, a pattern was beginning to emerge. Four of the seven candidates stood out. She was looking forward to meeting them face-to-face to probe further and narrow down to the top two she would recommend to the board.

Face to Face

Michelle conducted the interviews at the Plax offices. The venue was agreed upon in a bid to avoid triggering staff speculation about what was going on. Conducting interviews at PTI Industries' office might have caused undue anxiety among technical staff, as they had not yet been informed about Mark's forthcoming departure.

Bob Muro

The first candidate that Michelle met was the head of sales and marketing, Bob Muro. He was a gentleman you couldn't ignore - muscular, flamboyant, and with regular bursts of laughter that seemed to rock the room. Past the physical appearances, Michelle found him highly intense in his conversation, intelligent and knowledgeable. He however appeared confident to a level that Michelle thought bordered on arrogance.

Bob had been with the company for fifteen years. In the early days, he handled the sales and marketing function with the help of only one assistant. Over the years he had grown the team which now numbered a hundred and ten. Bob did not bother to hide his ambitions and interest in the top position.

As Michelle conversed with Bob, she realized that her perception of him as being arrogant was erroneous. He was fairly likeable and demonstrated a thorough understanding of the company. Viable candidate, she had to admit.

Shirley Asali

Next came Shirley Asali, head of HR. She was the self-assured diplomat and a stickler for details. In her fourth year at PTI Industries, she was well cut out for her current role, with consistently above average performance bearing testimony to this. As Michelle conversed with her, however, she quickly became aware of Shirley's glaring lack of a big-picture mindset which the company currently needed at the CEO level.

Jeremy Sani

Jeremy Sani, head of production, was interviewed next. He had an air of confidence and self-assurance that reminded Michelle of a wise, likeable and good natured uncle. Michelle noted that unlike Bob, Jeremy didn't go out of his way to try and impress. He had a 'take me or leave me' manner about him. Furthermore, he demonstrated an extremely good understanding of the company's overall potential, and gave suggestions on what could be changed to enable the company to correct its course and regain its market leadership. He impressed Michelle with his ideas about making some product and market-related changes, especially with regards to which foreign markets PTI Industries should consider expanding into, and giving well-founded reasons for avoiding others.

What Michelle did not know was that Jeremy had embarked on an intensive self-development journey after he was fired from his first job. Back then, he was young and naïve and behaved as though the world owed him. He had graduated from university with top honors in an engineering degree, specializing in manufacturing. Two months into his employment he approached his boss about a pay rise. He grumbled that he was doing much, much more than what he was being paid for. Unfortunately for him, several people in his department had been complaining about his unwillingness to work as part of a team. When his boss asked him about it, Jeremy shrugged his shoulders and said that some of his colleagues were not qualified enough academically to work there, let alone to be helped by someone with top-of-the-class qualifications like his. The last straw came a week later when Jeremy was asked to go to the office over a weekend to resolve a client's technical issue. He adamantly refused, saying that his salary had not been adjusted when he asked for a review. Early the following week the client withdrew their business, costing Jeremy's employer the equivalent of millions of dollars in lost revenue. Jeremy was fired the same day.

First Mentor

After staying out of a job for three months, an old family friend gave him a temporary position. It was there where he met Peter Sage who was to become his mentor of many years. Peter literally took him under his wings and taught Jeremy what he considered as his first real leadership lesson; before you attempt to lead others, you need to lead 'self' first. That turned out to be tougher than he had initially thought as he quickly found out that the hardest person to lead is always yourself. Previously, this had never occurred to him and he wondered why. His mentor helped him to understand that there is the tendency to judge oneself based on one's best intentions, while judging others based on their worst actions.

With Peter's help, Jeremy immediately started working on developing himself as a leader. By the time his temporary assignment came to an end six months later, he had developed a personal growth plan and got down to implementing it. He promised himself that he would become a topnotch leader, which he defined as learning to lead himself as best he could without making excuses for any shortcomings. That was also when he started drawing analogies between running a marathon and developing oneself as a leader.

He developed this self-leadership principle from the fact that in a marathon, you do not depend on the competencies of others. Rather, you develop yourself individually before going out to compete with others.

Jeremy got another job immediately after his temporary one ended, and from then on he became quite ruthless in developing himself. He had since come a long way, including a three-year posting overseas at the conclusion of which he joined PTI Industries.

Shortlist

The fourth candidate would have been the CIO, Jake Bima. However, he had withdrawn his candidacy at the very last minute, citing undisclosed personal reasons.

Thankfully, this move didn't jeopardize the process because Michelle already had two strong candidates in Bob and Jeremy.

Two days later, Michelle briefed Madam P on the outcome of the recruitment exercise. She outlined the process she had followed, her findings, the interview sessions, and eventual zeroing down to the two final candidates.

"In addition to the face-to-face interviews, we carried out psychometric tests for Bob and Jeremy. Interestingly, the two of them are strong, albeit in different ways." She paused to flip through her notes and pulled out a single sheet of paper which she smoothly slid across the desk to Madame P.

The header on the paper read, 'PTI Industries: CEO Search – Summary'. Below that was a table with three columns and several rows. The columns were labeled 'Competency', 'Jeremy' and 'Bob', respectively. For each competency, there were several bullet points under each of the candidates' names.

Only giving Madam P time to glance at the notes, Michelle continued speaking. "Both candidates have above-average rankings in all the areas we were considering. The main difference lies in their people skills. They both ranked strongly in vision, but then Jeremy exhibited distinctly higher people skills than Bob. The final step in the process will be to run an independent test for the two candidates."

Madam P wanted to know by what means they would confirm who seemed a better fit for the position.

Michelle had a ready answer, "I suggest we take the pulse of the staff members as they are important stakeholders in the process. This can be done easily through a poll disguised as a staff survey, with select questions aimed at gathering additional information on the candidates."

Madam P was doubtful, "Wouldn't it be subject to bias?"

"Handled correctly, it will not. We have used it successfully with several clients over the last ten years."

Madam P still wasn't convinced.

"It is an in-house tool we developed and we took it through rigorous testing after development. It measures candidates along 97 percent of the leadership attributes we were considering in the short-listing and interviewing stages of the recruitment process. It serves as an independent check of our findings and is administered as a confidential staff survey," Michelle said confidently.

"Oh, I see" said Madam P. "My main concern is about ensuring objectivity without compromising the integrity of the outcome. If that is taken care of, let's proceed with the survey and meet again in one and a half weeks' time for a final briefing."

Poll

Exactly a week and a half later, Michelle held the follow up meeting with Madam P and two other board members who had expertise in HR and strategy respectively. She had analyzed the results from the polling exercise, and now presented them to the group.

"Out of 1,200 employees who were invited to take part in the survey, 1,041 responded. That is an 87 percent response rate, which is impressive for a poll conducted at such short notice.

"Of the 1,041 respondents: 6 percent of the votes were spoilt; 34 percent rated Bob highly as an effective leader; and 60 percent voted for Jeremy. That gives us a clear lead," Michelle summed up.

For the next hour, the board members discussed the two candidates at length. They invited Bob and Jeremy in turns to the meeting and asked some clarifying questions. Finally, they agreed that Jeremy had sufficiently demonstrated ability in leadership attributes which they considered a high priority for the CEO job. They agreed to put his name forward to the full board for ratification as the new CEO.

On a sunny Thursday afternoon a couple of days later, the board met at the office. The mood was light, in stark contrast to the last meeting. The chair of the finance and HR committee briefed members on the recruitment exercise, and concluded with the recommendation for Jeremy's appointment. It was passed unanimously. That being the main business for the day, the meeting was adjourned shortly thereafter.

Blow

Madam P stopped by Mark's office to brief him on the outcome of the meeting. He had not been invited, given that the agenda was the discussion of his successor. After a quick greeting, she immediately said what had brought her in.

"I know you were not expecting me, but thought it best that you hear the news directly from me," she started.

"Oh, I appreciate that," Mark responded.

Madam P did not miss the slight uneasiness in his voice, but given that she had already started the conversation, she reasoned that she might as well continue. In any case, someone would have had to handle the delicate announcement. She however decided that the less said, the better, and proceeded as gently as she could, "After a rigorous search process, the executive search firm identified potential internal candidates to carry on the work you've been doing. These were further considered by the board, resulting in the appointment of Jeremy as the next-in-line."

There was an audible gasp from Mark, though he looked composed. Madam P decided not to say anything more, wished Mark a good evening, and excused herself.

Left alone, Mark felt hot, cold, and hot again. The turn of events in just a few short weeks made him feel faint. The thought of Jeremy becoming his successor appeared to be the last straw as that meant he would have to be in close contact with him over the next several weeks for the hand over.

The earlier irritation he had felt towards Jeremy subsequent to their conversation several months before resurfaced and slowly metamorphosed into resentment. Even though the sun had not set and the day was still warm, he felt icy on the inside.

He began to dread the handover stage of his transition which was scheduled to begin the very next Monday afternoon. Mark was honest with himself and admitted that the thought of having to act civil to Jeremy would be difficult. However, he didn't have a choice and would therefore go through with it.

He decided it would be best to keep his contact with Jeremy during the transition period minimal. He wasn't going to trip over himself assisting. *If Jeremy struggles after that, let him learn from the famous school of 'hard knocks',* he thought. It would be a fine lesson for Jeremy to realize that he, too, could do with the advice he had readily dished out to Mark not too long before.

Mark even imagined a false sense of revenge should Jeremy not succeed in his new role. Deep down he knew he was reacting unkindly to Jeremy's success. But the thoughts served to distract him from thinking about a doctor's review for his wife, which was scheduled for that evening. He was accompanying Alison to the doctor's.

She had been going through a battery of tests. Initial test results were worrying, and now Mark found himself dreading the looming visit.

News of the Appointment

That evening, Madam P telephoned Jeremy. He had been out of the office the whole week, attending a conference at the coastal city of Mombasa.

The call found Jeremy in deep reflection on the balcony of his hotel room, overlooking the ocean. The sound of waves crashing onto the shore always had such a calming effect on him, making him feel one with nature.

"Congratulations, Jeremy!" Madam P said jovially.

Jeremy was about to ask why she was congratulating him but stopped just in time, *"Could it possibly be?"* he thought, his mind flashing back to the recent recruitment process. Since Mark's resignation, he had entertained the possibility of ascending to the CEO position. However, he hadn't allowed himself the luxury of getting too hopeful in case he was unsuccessful.

Madam P's voice cut into his thoughts, "This afternoon, the board confirmed your appointment as the next CEO. That's no mean achievement, and you've rightly earned it. We're all greatly looking forward to working closely with you."

"Thank you for sharing the good news, and the warm wishes," Mark said breathlessly, basking in the moment.

Not that he had any ill feelings towards Mark or that he wanted to gloat over his apparent failure and dismissal. Jeremy just saw this as an opportunity to implement some ideas that he reasoned could help turn the organization around and drive growth. Ever since his awkward conversation with Mark, he had eliminated all illusions about any of his ideas being welcomed by his now outgoing boss.

"It will be an honor for me to build PTI Industries with such an able team!" Jeremy beamed, and then informed Madam P that he still had another day of meetings and therefore would be back in the office on Monday.

"Your return date works perfectly, because Mark and I agreed that the handover process will kick off with a briefing that very afternoon," Madam P said. "I'll be in attendance," she finished off, and bade Jeremy goodbye. Getting off the phone, Jeremy immediately called his wife, Tanya, to convey the news.

"Sweetheart, that's the best news this year!" Tanya gushed with excitement. "I know you'll do really well in the job. And remember, I'll always be your best cheer-leader!"

"Don't I know it?" Jeremy responded eagerly. "This is just the beginning, though. The hard work is about to begin and I'm so grateful for your unwavering support."

After that Jeremy tried some light reading but finding it difficult to concentrate, he decided to have an early night. That turned out to be an unwise decision as he kept tossing and turning, torn hopelessly between anticipation and apprehension over his new role. He finally fell into a fitful sleep.

Jeremy's last day of meetings appeared to drag, as he toyed with the idea of calling Mark. He wanted to reconfirm the commencement of the handover process. In fact, it was a veiled attempt to be the first one to reach out in what he anticipated might be a season plagued by awkward moments between him and Mark. He knew it would be uncomfortable for both of them and finally let the idea go.

He was relieved when Mark called late in the afternoon. Their conversation was brief and uneasy, with Mark congratulating him and reconfirming the kickoff of the handover process.

While the call helped break the ice it didn't wipe out Jeremy's apprehension of what to expect over the next month or so. The weekend that followed appeared long.

Staff Announcement

In the meantime, an announcement was sent out to all staff regarding the leadership transition. Some employees had already got wind of the impending changes and the rumor mill was abuzz with speculation. Different members of the executive team were being proposed as possible successors, making matters confusing and resulting in some anxious moments. The confirmation was therefore timely.

There was quiet celebration among staff. Many had become discontent with Mark yet they did not want to be seen to be openly celebrating. Mark was still going to be around for several weeks anyway, and no one was too enthusiastic about souring relationships with him over the matter. They hoped that the changes signaled a new dawn for the company. Only time would tell.

The News

Finally, the day Jeremy would start working alongside Mark arrived! He got to the office early, and was greeted by warm smiles and congratulatory messages from staff. While silently pleased with the employees' obvious acceptance of his appointment, he hoped this would not place him in a difficult position with Mark.

Having been away for most of the previous week, there was a lot waiting for Jeremy's attention. Soon his office was a hive of activity with several meetings and calls, and Jeremy found himself struggling to keep up. He had to quietly slip out of his office and walk round the building a couple of times to stop himself from getting overwhelmed.

Shortly after returning from one such break, Jeremy's assistant buzzed to say there was an urgent call from Madam P. As she put the call through, Jeremy looked at his watch and realized it was a quarter past noon. *Not much time before the meeting with Mark,* he quietly thought to himself as Madame P's greeting came through the line.

"Have you heard the news?" She sounded edgy.

"What news?" Jeremy inquired.

"I just got off the phone with Mark. He called to inform me that he is taking urgent leave from the office with immediate effect. Apparently, his wife Alison has been diagnosed with cancer. This was confirmed to them last Thursday, following a series of tests that she has been going through," said Madam P.

Jeremy groaned. He knew Alison well, and also knew how much Mark adored her. In recent months, Mark had been lamenting that he just didn't seem to have time for her anymore. "That must be a huge blow to them," Jeremy said quietly, almost to himself.

"They are devastated," said Madam P. "They discussed treatment options with their doctor upon receipt of the results. After considering alternatives, they decided to seek specialized treatment abroad and immediately contacted a cancer treatment center they were referred to. They got word this morning that Alison can get admission immediately. The local doctor has advised that the sooner Alison gets started on treatment, the better the prognosis. Mark will be accompanying her, and they anticipate traveling by the end of the week.

"As you can imagine, our afternoon's planned meeting with Mark has taken a back seat as far as he's concerned. He regrets that he will not return to the office until after their trip. Depending on how treatment goes, who knows when that might be." Madam P let the statement hang in the air.

Jeremy reeled with shock from the double blow. The news about Alison's diagnosis was bad enough. Now the realization that he would be thrust into his new position without any formal handover made the prospects of success look bleak. Worse still, he would have to juggle his new role with his current responsibilities as head of production since his deputy, Maureen Kasum was only six months into the job and lacked the capacity to take charge immediately. Even if someone was to be recruited to replace him, that would take time. Whichever way he looked at it, his elevation to CEO position seemed more intimidating than inviting. This was definitely not what he had envisioned when he accepted the challenge.

"Welcome to the real world!" Madam P's voice cut through Jeremy's thoughts.

"Sure, I guess this is as real as it gets with the new turf!" Jeremy chuckled nervously, trying hard to gain composure.

"One of my mentors' personal mantra is that it is the leader's responsibility to define reality," Jeremy recalled. "What's the reality of this situation? Mark is off the scene. I'm new in office and need to learn the ropes. PTI Industries has to continue." It was as if he was ticking items off a checklist.

Madam P tried to encourage him, "We have a new CEO, a fairly strong executive team, and a functioning board."

"You're right. We have more working for us than against us," said Jeremy, sounding more confident after that exchange. "Let's start with an executive briefing on the current situation, and then map a way forward."

Madam P appreciated Jeremy's decisiveness. "Since I am available this afternoon, we can have the briefing in place of the handover kickoff."

That afternoon, Jeremy and Madam P held a hurriedly convened meeting with members of the executive team. In attendance was Jeremy, Bob, Shirley, Jake, Ryan Mose, who was head of corporate communications, Helen Kale, the legal counsel, Nancy Bobo, the CFO and Olivia Lima, head of strategy.

Madam P kicked off the meeting, "Good afternoon, ladies and gentlemen. I sincerely appreciate your making time to meet at such short notice. We'll keep it brief."

"You've already received email on part of what I'm about to say, but I'll repeat it because nothing beats face to face communication. As you know, after many years of dedicated service to the company, Mark recently resigned. We immediately engaged a recruiter to help us fill the position. Thankfully, the process was smooth and ended up with the identification of the next CEO." Turning to Jeremy with a broad smile, she said slowly, "Would you, please, join me in wishing many years of success to Jeremy Sani in his new role!" Her announcement was met with applause from all but Jeremy and Bob. The latter appeared a little aloof, which was understandable as he had been extremely hopeful of getting the job. Madam P let his silence pass.

She then briefed the team on Mark's abrupt departure and appealed to them to give Jeremy every support he would need to transition successfully. After that she asked Jeremy if he had anything to say.

He too, was brief. "Thank you for your warm wishes. We've come a long way together, and now I look forward to working even more closely with each of you as we shape the future of this great company." "Together, we can turn the company onto the profitability path. Together, we will do it!" He punched the air with his fist as the team, with the exception of Bob, clapped.

The meeting ended and Jeremy walked out of the conference room with a smile on his face. He knew he had fairly good working relations with individual members of the executive team and was therefore confident that the journey ahead would be smooth.

Little did he know.

The key lessons I learned in this chapter

The action steps I will take as a result

CHAPTER 4

BALANCE

Balance is not something you find, it's something you create.
Jana Kingsford

Striking a Balance During Transition

Over the first few days in his new role, Jeremy found himself stretched to the limit.

Colleagues steadily stopped by his office to congratulate and offer him best wishes. He was in the office long before everyone else and left well after nightfall. With each passing day, however, the reality of balancing his previous role and stepping up into his new position began to sink in.

It was a delicate dance between the cordial, the operational and the strategic. He quickly realized that if he didn't put a system in place, it was just a matter of time before things started to fall through the cracks.

So he worked with his personal assistant, Enid, to manage the flow of visitors and limit interruptions to brief breaks from work. Bubbly thirty-five-year-old Enid had also served as Mark's PA, and Jeremy made the decision to keep her. She knew the office well, she was business savvy, and she struck a good balance between maturity and relationships. Enid was exactly what Jeremy needed to manage the day-to-day affairs while he settled in. Jeremy scheduled twice-daily briefings with Maureen where he was apprised of production operations and he provided guidance on keeping the business unit running as smoothly as possible. In between meetings, he was available for consultations on urgent matters requiring his direct involvement.

The new position, however, was his biggest stretch. To lead effectively, he knew he needed to learn as much as possible rather than assume that he knew the company and had all the answers. One of his confidantes, his local pastor named Martin, frequently told him, "Before you make any significant changes or decisions in any new situation, it's best to adopt an attitude of openness, curiosity and learning."

He realized that taking this approach now would help him reconfirm what he already knew about the staff and company, and also open up areas that he did not know about. It would be worthwhile having one-on-one briefings with executive team members and a few other staff drawn from different departments and levels. The latter would give him feedback from the front-lines on the company's performance. He also held a few breakfast briefings with the company's major clients. He deemed it important for an outside-in view of the business.

Over the next one and a half weeks, Jeremy listened more than he spoke. He asked a lot of questions, paid attention and took notes. He reviewed operational and financial reports, in the process reconfirming what he already knew; the company was not doing well. He was confident, however, that the situation could be turned around with careful planning and dedicated execution. But this would only happen if every employee played their part well and supported others on their teams. There was no room for anyone to be slothful or fail to perform to expectations.

This made a finding on his last day of meetings significant. It happened when he met with the sales manager, Mimi Monashi, who shared information that cast a dark cloud on the bright and sunny Wednesday morning.

The Allegation

Previously, Jeremy and Mimi had never had close interactions, as Jeremy dealt more with Mimi's boss, Bob. He was therefore taken aback when halfway through their discussions, Mimi leaned forward and said in a somewhat conspiratorial manner, "I think there's something you need to know about my boss." She was referring to Bob Muro.

Jeremy was not one to encourage backstabbing. He was instinctively going to tell Mimi to stick to issues, not personalities, and then change the subject to drive his point home. However, there was a note of sincerity in Mimi's voice that caught his attention. He was curious. All the same, he decided to play it safe and therefore asked in a tone that bordered on indifference, "Oh, what is that?"

"As you know, sales and marketing has been running a series of promotions to push out old stock." Jeremy nodded. Mimi continued, "Part of the promotions have involved aggressive selling to our retailers. In addition, even though PTI Industries now distributes directly on the retail market, we decided to select a few wholesalers we previously worked with and give them attractive discounts to entice them to distribute our products to their networks.

"When I was reviewing the sales report for the last quarter, I got curious about a new distributor called Pallam & Associates that has been receiving huge discounts. When we used to work with a small network of wholesalers, Pallam & Associates were not on that list of distributors. I found out that the discounts had been approved by Bob and that none of my direct reports had any information about the distributor. I decided to do a little search in case Bob's approval was an oversight and I needed to bring the fact to his attention.

"I contacted the wholesaler directly to inquire who had introduced them to PTI Industries, but they seemed cagey. On four different occasions when I telephoned them, I was kept on hold or was tossed from one extension to another, and then the call would be abruptly disconnected. That got me more than a little curious. But I also realized I needed to change my approach."

Jeremy didn't interrupt, so Mimi went on, "Using a contact I have at the Registrar of Companies' office, I found out that the majority shareholder, who is also a non-executive director of Pallam & Associates, goes by the name Robert Muro. I quickly put two and two together and concluded that it is no doubt Bob—our Bob."

Jeremy's heart raced. Nonetheless, he realized he couldn't afford to jump to conclusions too quickly and start chasing after red herrings. Surely, that name Bob was not unique to PTI Industries? However, he knew at the back of his mind that if Bob was the same person behind the company, it would amount to grave conflict of interest. This could not be taken lightly for someone at his level.

After a moment's silence, he asked, "Have you asked Bob about the dealer? Even if he is the Robert in those records, there's possibly a very simple explanation to all that."

"No, I haven't asked Bob. It would be awkward for me since I report directly to him. He might think I'm undermining him, especially if it turned out that either you or Mike knew about the matter," Mimi said.

"Okay. Leave that information with me and don't mention it to anyone else for now," Jeremy said.

Tight Spot

Alone in his office later that evening, Jeremy looked out of the window and saw the setting sun looking like a startling splash of red and orange colors. It momentarily dazzled his eyes but it moved quickly as it sank lower in the horizon. It would soon be dark. Struggling to get over the sudden feeling of discouragement in light of the information he had received that morning, he drew hope from the fact that even if the sun was going down, it would be up again the following morning. *After darkness that comes with nighttime, the day breaks,* he thought. *Even matters at PTI Industries will clear.*

All the same, he quietly wondered what he should do with the newly acquired information. That it involved Bob did not help matters. He needed to tread carefully and not come out pointing an accusing finger at him.

If he brought the matter out in the open and it turned out to be another Robert, matters could blow up in his face. He would be seen to be pursuing a personal agenda of trying to discredit Bob and he would lose credibility with his team. If, on the other hand, the assertion was true, what measures should he take? Sack Bob? A public investigation against a senior employee who had just faced off with him in the recent interviews could easily be interpreted as a witch-hunt to weaken his strongest challenger.

He wondered why this, of all matters, had to land on his desk now. What a welcome to his new role! He had assumed that being CEO would take him above petty issues. He had to admit to himself though that this was not a trivial issue since it was potentially a legal matter involving violation of the conflict of interest policy by a senior company official.

He couldn't ask Shirley in HR to investigate. She and Bob were good friends. If the claim turned out to be true, Jeremy felt he didn't know Shirley well enough to take comfort in her impartiality. She could be easily tempted to look for ways of shading the truth so as to protect Bob.

It was also a pity he couldn't call Mark for advice. A legal company issue would be the last thing to bother Mark with as he faced his wife's life-and-death situation.

Jeremy thought of calling his old friend and mentor, Eric Lone. Immediately, he dismissed the idea. Eric was currently vacationing in Australia and Jeremy knew Eric well enough to appreciate that supportive as he was of Jeremy, he wouldn't take an interruption to his first real holiday in four years kindly. Eric's company had just completed a drawn-out, hostile takeover of a rival firm and as CEO, he had been sucked into the legal and professional battles both mentally and emotionally. Eric had complained about total burnout and clearly needed the break.

Jeremy momentarily reminisced about their relationship through the years. He had met Eric through a mutual friend, about two years before the passing on of his first mentor, Peter Sage. They hit it off immediately. Eric was in the process of selling off his first company, after having started his second one. Back then, Eric would meet with Jeremy once every quarter. Each time, Eric would regale him with stories of friends and acquaintances who had started businesses, burnt their fingers in the process but kept trying again and again until they succeeded. There was a common theme of hard work and persistence in each one.

After Eric's second business took off successfully, he had more time on his hands and the frequency of their meetings increased to once a month. His stories continued to revolve around business lessons. Lifting up three fingers for emphasis, he would often say, "Three things you must do to build a successful business – foster relationships, seize opportunities as they come, and learn to ask great questions."

Eric also served as the voice of caution or encouragement to Jeremy in both personal and professional matters. Even when Jeremy got an overseas posting for three years, the two kept in touch.

When Jeremy returned to the country to join PTI Industries, they started quarterly face-to-face half-day mentoring meetings. Over the last couple of years, though, they had met only twice because of Eric's time constraints.

Eric had celebrated every significant achievement in Jeremy's life, and supported him through every major setback. Giving Eric the space to enjoy his time out and waiting to speak with him in person was the least Jeremy could do to honor Eric's enduring guidance and backing over the years.

That of course meant he would have to turn to another advisor. *Who can I talk to?* He wondered. Continuing with his reflections, a thought crossed his mind. *What would the board's role in a matter like this be? At what point should it be roped in?* He remembered some of Eric's many lessons on board matters. His all-time favorite was one about the wisdom in making board members allies, instead of alienating and antagonizing them. He wondered what that meant in the current situation. The more he thought about it, the more he realized the need to bring Madam P into the picture. It was the least he could do as the issue at hand bordered on governance.

Looking at his watch, he realized it was already getting to eight o'clock. He dialed Madam P's number and waited for only a couple of rings before she picked up.

"My sincere apologies for calling late," Jeremy started.

Madam P promptly interrupted him. "It must be important, so no need to apologize."

"It *is* important," Jeremy assured her and dove right into the matter. He briefed her on the situation.

Madam P listened without interrupting and when Jeremy was done, she said quietly, as if thinking aloud, "You know how potentially explosive this is. It will of course be necessary to investigate the assertion, which could turn out either way."

Jeremy instinctively nodded, but stopped abruptly as he remembered that this was a telephone conversation. He quickly said, "And either outcome has implications." It was obvious to both that whatever action would be taken needed to be handled with sensitivity.

If Bob found out he was being investigated and it turned out the claim had no substance, relations between them would be badly damaged. On the other hand, if the suspicion turned out to be true, the consequences could be far-reaching.

They agreed to first gather as much information about the distributor as possible without attracting undue attention. They would then ascertain any links with Bob and if proved true, determine the course of action consistent with the conflict of interest policy. To do all this, they would need to enlist assistance of Helen from the legal office. Madam P was scheduled to travel out of the country the following day, so they agreed to review progress in the coming week.

Background Check

The next morning, Jeremy briefed Helen in confidence about the allegations.

"Helen, I cannot repeat enough times how important it is to uphold utmost confidentiality in the investigation," he concluded gravely.

Helen swung into action immediately. On Tuesday morning of the following week, she called Jeremy to propose a meeting, "We've made good progress, and I would like to update you on what we've gathered." They met later that morning.

"I got my assistant to gather information on the distributor without raising any suspicions." Helen began. "She reconfirmed the initial findings that Robert Muro is one of the company's shareholders and directors. What's more, the contact details and signatures in documents at the Registrar of Companies' office are similar to what we have in Bob's personnel file here," she continued. "So clearly there's gross conflict of interest violation because Bob co-owns a company that's doing business with PTI Industries, is significantly benefiting from this relationship, and yet he hasn't disclosed his interest."

"What are the implications of a conflict of interest violation by an executive team member?" asked Jeremy.

"Outright dismissal," Helen responded without hesitation.

After thoughtful consideration, Jeremy said "In that case, we don't have room for mistakes."

"I'm afraid not." Helen agreed.

The two agreed to brief Madam P via teleconference later in the day.

This happened in the afternoon. Jeremy and Helen apprised Madam P on findings, then the three discussed possible alternatives for following up on the matter. They agreed to engage a private investigator who would interview all parties concerned and peruse documents without raising suspicions. They would also ascertain if other staff were involved and in what capacity.

Three weeks later, the three sat together with the full board in the company's boardroom. Before them was a report from the private investigator, confirming that Bob was the brains behind the company in question. No other employees were involved. The board discussed at length the facts of the case, the conflict of interest policy and the implications of Bob's actions. Unanimously, all agreed that he would have to be let go immediately. It would be the second senior sacking within months, making it a delicate exercise.

To mitigate against the possibility of staff feeling insecure and jittery about their jobs, a memo would be sent out as soon as Bob was released. It would highlight circumstances surrounding his departure: the initial allegations–without explaining how these came forth, so as to protect Mimi–the thorough and independent investigation, and the outcome.

The key lessons I learned in this chapter

The action steps I will take as a result

CHAPTER 5

SECOND EXIT

Sort of like a turtle – tough on the outside, tender on the inside.
Anonymous

Meeting Before The Meeting

That settled, the next step was to present Bob with the findings. The board agreed that Jeremy, Madam P and Helen should handle the matter. The three remained behind after all the other board members left, and discussed a plan of action. They agreed to face up to Bob the following morning.

Jeremy buzzed Bob. "Hey Bob, there's an important matter I'd like to discuss with you tomorrow morning. Please make room in your schedule to meet at ten."

"I have an important client meeting at ten-thirty. How long will the discussion take?" Bob sounded hurried.

Jeremy was noncommittal "It's hard to tell. Ask someone else on your team to sit in with the client."

Bob hesitated a moment and then said, as if partly thinking aloud, "I'll see if I can push it earlier, which is what the client preferred in the first place. But there's an analysis to be completed before then. I suppose my assistant can work late today to complete the background work to make it possible for us to have the client meeting first thing tomorrow. "Okay, then. Ten o'clock confirmed."

"I appreciate your flexibility, Bob." Jeremy's voice did not betray any emotion.

After Jeremy got off the phone with Bob, he turned to the other two and said, "We need to bring HR into the loop. After all, Shirley will be the one managing the exit process so she needs to be in the picture." As they nodded their heads, he continued, "Knowing Shirley and her relationship with Bob, we shouldn't brief her too early. I would say an hour before we meet with Bob is sufficient. That minimizes the risk of Bob getting wind of the matter beforehand."

Dynamite

At a quarter to nine the next morning, the three congregated in the small conference room and went over the action plan one more time.

Five minutes to nine, Jeremy buzzed Shirley. "Shirley, I need to see you urgently. Could you come to the small conference room?" Two minutes later, Shirley strode into the room. She looked surprised to see Madame P and Helen also sitting around the table, but quickly pulled herself together. She shook hands politely and Jeremy motioned for her to sit down. She took a seat next to Helen, directly opposite Jeremy.

"We will dive right in," Jeremy said, looking at Shirley. "I'll begin with some background information to provide context to what I'll be sharing. Recently, my office received an anonymous tip-off about some irregularity involving a new distributor of PTI Industries and a senior member of staff."

He went on to explain that in consultation with the board, a decision was made to use the services of a private investigator, in order to ensure that a totally objective process was followed and to protect the employee's reputation should the claim turn out to be baseless. The process was now complete and had revealed grievous conflict of interest on the employee's part. "We have no alternative but to immediately release the executive concerned," he concluded.

Question marks were written all over Shirley's face, but she listened without interrupting.

Jeremy went on, "The senior employee we're talking about is Bob Muro."

Shirley exploded, her eyes flashing with a mixture of shock and anger. "How come no one informed me about the investigation? Surely as the person in charge of HR I should have been involved from the beginning? In any case, how sure can I be that HR policies were not flouted? How can you prove that there was objectivity in the process and that this was not just a personal vendetta?" The latter statement was a veiled accusation that Jeremy was possibly attempting to get rid of a prospective contestant.

Madam P, who had been silent all along, now calmly spoke up. "It's important that we keep facts and fiction separate. This is an organizational matter and *not* a personal issue." She paused for effect and then said, "Members of the board have been involved from early on in the process, and can vouch for its objectivity." She delved into details of the process followed and concluded by saying, "Great effort was taken to ensure a fair process. As head of HR, we are counting on you to facilitate the exit process."

Shirley groped for loopholes in the process. "But has Bob been given a chance to explain his position?"

Madam P had a ready answer. "The exit will not happen until we give Bob a fair hearing to justify his actions. We are meeting with him in the next hour, and would like you to sit in and make your own independent judgment."

Shirley shrugged her shoulders, but did not protest further.

A discussion ensued on the need to include a session on the roles and responsibilities of directors at the next executive retreat. Shirley was mainly quiet and thoughtful. The discussion went on till a couple of minutes after ten o'clock, when Bob strode into the conference room.

Bombshell

Like Shirley before him, Bob seemed surprised to see the group seated there. The spring in his step was replaced by a more hesitant gait, but his face gave no indication as to whether he suspected what the meeting was about.

"I didn't know it was a group meeting," Bob said as he shook hands with Madam P, nodded at the rest and took the only remaining seat, between Shirley and Madam P.

"Well, yes it is." Jeremy said, looking at Bob. "We have a weighty matter to discuss, which is best presented by different stakeholders."

Jeremy wasted no time, "A few weeks ago, we received a serious allegation which was leveled against you." He watched for any reactions from Bob, who remained straight-faced. "Well, we decided that it was in both your, and the company's, interests to investigate it confidentially as it could have turned out either way—unfounded or true. So we engaged the services of a private investigator who has recently submitted a report confirming the initial allegations.

"Reportedly, you are a majority shareholder and director of Pallam & Associates, a wholesaler." Bob nodded, but didn't say anything.

"We also know that Pallam & Associates is a new distributor of PTI Industries products, and has been receiving huge discounts in that regard. This is against policy for new distributors. The fact that you have considerable interests in Pallam & Associates amounts to significant conflict of interest on your part." Jeremy looked at Bob, motioning to him to respond.

There was a short awkward silence, and then Bob bristled, "You're challenging my integrity."

"Not yet. At least, not directly." Jeremy said. "We are interested in hearing your side of the story."

Bob looked cornered, and shifted uncomfortably in his seat. He fumbled for words, and then seemed to change his mind about whatever he was going to say. Finally, he smiled sheepishly and said, "We've been through such a busy period, the matter completely escaped my mind. I meant to talk it over with Mark, but he left suddenly. His departure was of course followed by the transition period and as I gave you–Jeremy–time to settle down, we got even busier on the large scale promotion of pushing out old stock. As you can imagine, the last few months have been a rollercoaster ride for me.

"No harm intended. And now that the matter has come up before I got an opportunity to bring it up myself, I do hope you will excuse my oversight over this small matter. I'm sure we'll be able to sort it out amicably."

Bob paused briefly but before anyone could get a word in, he started talking about his substantial contribution to the company over the years, how he had sacrificed a lot to develop the sales and marketing division, and also how he played his part in helping position the company as a leading brand. He flashed a disarming smile and said, "I look forward to continue contributing in the building of this remarkable company."

Madam P didn't look impressed, but chose her words carefully. "We must give credit where it's due. True, you have played a significant role in building the company brand over the years. I heartily commend you for that and believe both management and the rest of the board will do no less."

Jeremy nodded as Madam P continued. "You are right in saying that we've been through a busy phase." She seemed to shift gears as she said, "However, we cannot overlook the seriousness of the matter at hand. And timing is no excuse. It's outright unethical and your position in the company makes it even worse."

Bob sat up straight, as if realizing that he was not going to get away so easily. "I can explain the timing. Several months before Mark left the company, I started thinking about taking early retirement and therefore registered my own company-Pallam & Associates. It was going to be my next stop. When I was given an opportunity to interview for the CEO job it was as if I got a new lease of life. My commitment to PTI Industries was renewed and I started re-thinking my earlier decision to leave. In the meantime, Pallam & Associates had started trading. In the midst of all that, it didn't occur to me that I should do something about Pallam & Associates, now that I wasn't going to leave so soon after all. A blind corner, which is unfortunate but one I'm sure you can understand and pardon."

Even *he* sounded unconvinced, which Madam P was quick to point out. "Bob, that does not even begin to explain how it is that you approved huge discounts to Pallam & Associates and yet forgot that you needed to do something about the change in plans. In any case, you ought to have disclosed your interests right from the beginning." She paused for a moment and then said with finality, "We do not wish to set a regrettable precedent that could limit our range of options in the future. There is simply no room for laxity. The conflict of interest policy is clear and regrettably, we'll have to let you go with immediate effect."

Bob changed tactics. He pleaded for leniency, saying that it was an unfortunate lapse in professional judgment. He said he had learned his lesson, and promised there would be no recurrence of a similar happening.

Madam P spoke up. "At the risk of repeating myself, let me say that the matter at hand is a grave one for any employee. That it has happened at the executive level makes it more serious. We owe it to this renowned company that you have helped build, and to its equally illustrious employees and customers, to uphold the standards of integrity which are the bedrock of all that we are and do. It would be unforgivable for us to set a regrettable precedence which would be difficult to uphold in the future."

Seeing that there was no let up, Bob said, "I have always hoped that I would never be driven to do what I realize I must do now. But it seems I have no choice. I have a dossier that is incriminating to the management and board of PTI Industries, and absolutely damaging to the company. I won't use it against you and the company if you let me stay. But if not, then I'm going straight to the press…" he trailed to see if his bait would catch.

Jeremy and Helen exchanged concerned looks, but Shirley only stared at Bob as if trying to weigh the seriousness of his statements. Madame P appeared unmoved and said coolly, "My only response to what sounds like attempted blackmail is that we cannot stop you from sharing the information you have with whoever you choose. We'll respond appropriately." Relief swept over Jeremy and Helen's faces.

Madam P then asked Shirley to work out Bob's severance package and facilitate his immediate separation from the company. At this, Bob stood up, shook his fist at no one in particular and shouted, "I'll be back!" His threat sounded hollow.

He walked out of the room, banging the door behind him.

Tough and Tender

Jeremy was tasked with communicating the circumstances of Bob's exit to staff. It was a delicate balance, as he needed to highlight the seriousness of the matter, without revealing too many unnecessary details.

He immediately called Ryan of corporate communications and briefed him accordingly. Ryan would draft the communication which would go out under Jeremy's signature the following morning.

Jeremy was grateful for having spent enough time around his mentor, Eric, to know that experiences such as this one came with the territory. He would just have to develop a thick skin and move with the flow, as this was only one of many battles he would have to fight in his new role. It was a step closer to what Eric often likened to being like a turtle—tough on the outside, tender on the inside.

Later that evening Jeremy mulled on his first couple of months as CEO. In between orientation briefings from his team and clients and handling the just concluded ethical challenge, he had spent considerable amounts of time in his old role. He had kept up a frenzied pace, and looked forward to the day he could settle down enough to feel on top of his game.

Life outside the office was not any easier. His three children, aged between thirteen and nineteen years, presented different challenges for him. They increasingly spent more time with friends and he felt increasingly shut out of what was going on. Yet, he yearned to continue influencing them significantly and help to shape their choices. It was as if he was constantly fighting to be included. That drained him.

With Eric busy and traveling, he didn't have a proper sounding board for his ideas, or a reliable accountability partner to help him maintain balance or nudge him along.

All of this made Jeremy feel hassled and empty. It was a far cry from the anticipation and excitement that had enveloped him when Madam P called to inform him about his appointment as CEO.

The key lessons I learned in this chapter

The action steps I will take as a result

CHAPTER 6

PARALLEL LEARNING PATH

Leadership and learning are indispensable to each other.
John F. Kennedy

Putting Things Into Perspective

As Jeremy was going through his steep learning curve, Mark was going through a different type of learning.

Providentially, he and his wife were able to travel abroad for Alison's treatment as originally planned. A day after their arrival, Alison was admitted at the cancer treatment center while Mark stayed at a local hotel just five miles away. Her treatment program began immediately.

With Alison undergoing various tests and procedures, Mark found himself with plenty of free time in between checking on her. Even though he previously enjoyed reading, he was finding it difficult to concentrate. His top pastimes now became taking walks around the hospital grounds and sitting by a stream which ran through the property. Both presented plenty of time to indulge in private thoughts and thus began his journey of self-reflection.

He thought about his separation from PTI Industries, his future career, family, friends and life in general. But mostly, he thought about Alison and the twenty-years of marriage they had enjoyed together. It hadn't been all bliss and they had their fair share of disagreements and fights, but overall, theirs had been a good union.

Watching her in hospital now made him realize how much he had taken her for granted in the name of building his career. Ironically, it was the same career that had come to a grinding halt–in his mind, at least–with his sacking. He desperately longed for another opportunity to make it up to Alison by intentionally setting aside more time for his family. Would he get a second chance?

One thing that dawned on him was how fragile life is. Thoughts about developing relationships with other people and making a positive difference in their lives filled him with a sense of urgency that he had never experienced before. During one of his lowest moments, he remembered a commencement address he had come across a while back that was attributed to Bryan Dyson, former chief operating officer of the Coca-Cola Company.

Though his memory was a bit hazy, he seemed to remember that the message was partly about imagining life as a game in which one juggles five balls in the air. The balls are named work, family, health, friends, and spirit, and one has to try and keep all the balls in the air.

Work is a rubber ball which when dropped, will bounce back. However, the four other balls–family, health, friends, and spirit–are made of glass. If any one of them is dropped, it will be irrevocably scuffed, marked, nicked, damaged or even shattered; it will never be the same. The message appealed for one to understand this lesson and strive for balance in life.

Mark felt a chill run down his spine. The message was so acutely relevant to his current situation. His priorities up to this point had been totally mixed up, and yet he had not realized it. *How could I have been so blind?*

The more Mark reflected on that message, the more his outlook on life was transformed. Finally, he was able to put his sacking from PTI Industries into perspective. Cast alongside Alison's sickness, it didn't seem such a big deal now.

The earlier grudge against Jeremy and the desire to exact a small measure of revenge also began to thaw. He realized now that he would have nothing to gain by watching Jeremy flounder and eventually follow in his footsteps to failure. After all, Jeremy was not the cause of his misstep. Rather, a combination of errors of judgment and negligence on his part had resulted in his failing to deliver on his mandate as CEO.

All this reflection resulted in Mark resolving to do everything within his power to help Jeremy avoid the pitfalls that had led to his own downfall. He would seek Jeremy out on his return home and support him in whatever way possible. And so began a new chapter in his life.

Quarter One Results

Back at PTI Industries, the board was staring at a grim picture. They were reviewing the company's performance for the first time since Mark's departure. The financial results for the quarter were poor.

"How do you explain this?" Madame P asked Jeremy immediately after he tabled the results.

With all the happenings since taking office, Jeremy had suspected that the results would be unspectacular. However, he had hoped that they would be much better than the picture staring at him now. Indeed, he had agonized over what he was going to say to the board since the previous week when the CFO presented the reports to him.

Looking round the room, he wiped his brow apprehensively and said, "As you know, we've been through a rough stretch. Mark's sudden departure and my rushed transition did not provide the stability I needed to get a good grip on things quickly." He shuffled the papers he was holding, "I'm finally settling into my role, and anticipate a better quarter ahead."

Madam P said in an even tone, "We hope so. We understand the start has not been an easy one and for this reason we will not be too hard on you. However, there are shareholders' interests at stake. We hired you because we had confidence that you could turn the situation around. Please don't disappoint us. We look forward to results, not reasons."

Jeremy felt harshly judged, but he kept his thoughts to himself. He resolved to work round the clock and exceed the board's expectations. *The board members will be in for a surprise come next meeting*, he promised himself.

He could not have known the surprise that awaited him.

Reset

For several days after the board meeting, Jeremy reflected a lot on feedback he had received through his briefings with staff and clients. He convened another meeting, this time with his executive team.

"Even though the last quarter was a difficult one for us, I'm confident that the next one will be easier. The very helpful suggestions that you and others shared recently have greatly informed what I'm about to share.

"I strongly believe we should reposition the company by re-launching some product lines, discontinuing a few, and targeting overseas customers."

Ryan was the first to respond, "I won't pretend to be a strategist, but you all know that my work involves reviewing a lot of internal and external reports. Some of them give useful indications about what a number of our competitors are up to. What Jeremy is proposing will enable us stand out in our industry." His comments were received with understanding nods, so Jeremy continued, "It is also clear that all of us in this room should be more intentional about developing ourselves and those we lead."

The team spent several minutes discussing how the ideas could be implemented, and identified who should take the lead on each action item.

Afterward, Jeremy shared his intentions to launch fortnightly staff gatherings, which he christened *'baraza'*. They would be forums for listening to comments from employees on what was happening on the frontlines and discussing how they could improve the company. He said that these and other ideas from staff would be put in place over time.

He wrapped up the meeting with the words, "I hope that your renewed sense of commitment and the positive energy which are evident will continue to build up. Let's keep the momentum!"

The Glitch

Barely two days later, his optimism was dealt a huge blow. This came during a review meeting with Maureen, deputy head of production.

She sounded agitated, "As you know, a month ago we started selling the new high performance precision instrument, the HPPI8-A." Jeremy knew the instrument only too well, having worked on it with his team for the better part of the previous year. Maureen continued, "To date, we have sold 15,000 units to customers who had pre-ordered it during the market testing phase of the product.

"Well yesterday, customer service informed me they had received complaints from ten different customers who purchased the instruments and today there were complaint calls from five more." Maureen relaxed a little, before the disturbed look returned, "I immediately got my team investigating the complaints."

Jeremy had a sinking feeling at the bottom of his stomach. He knew how long they had worked to develop the instrument and the extra hours that the team had put in, working into the evenings and over weekends. However, and against a recommendation from Maureen, he directed that they skip the extra pre-market test which was advisable for new high performance instruments.

Pressure

Jeremy took a mental trip back in time. The product development cycle for the HPPI8-A had been a lengthy, detailed process. A final independent check would have been ideal.

He had been under intense pressure from Mark who wouldn't hear of any further delays, and wanted the product on the market immediately. He was anxious to launch before a similar product that the competition was rumored to be importing from their overseas plant hit the market.

Bowing to pressure, and against his better judgment, Jeremy directed that they go ahead and produce one hundred thousand units in the first batch. The directive would return to haunt him.

Jeremy asked thoughtfully, "What are the findings so far?"

Maureen hesitated. "It's too early in the process. We have to do a thorough production system audit which could take weeks."

"Yes, of course," Jeremy replied. "I would appreciate your keeping me updated every couple of days. And if there is something significant to report, don't wait two days, just come right in."

Maureen committed to giving Jeremy regular updates and then exited the office, leaving him in deep thought.

More Reflection

For the next two hours or so, Jeremy found it difficult to concentrate. Just when he had felt ready to immerse himself in his 'not-so-new' role, the report about a possible fault in the company's latest product came. He tried to reassure himself that it could be merely a minor fault that required a simple adjustment on some of the units produced.

At the back of his mind, however, was the gnawing thought that it could turn out to be a major defect, in the same league as those that became case studies for business schools. If the latter proved the case, he knew he stood no chance of surviving as CEO, if the mood of the last board meeting was anything to go by. Much as the board empathized with him, Madam P had made it clear that they could not ignore the larger question of shareholders' interests. After weighing the matter in his mind, he decided that he would not be doing himself any favors by conveying news of the possible defect to Madam P at this time.

With each update from Maureen, over the next few weeks, it became clear that the problem was snowballing into a major product failure. It was an unprecedented snag in the history of PTI Industries.

The Blow

The crisis unfolded three and a half weeks later.

By this time, complaints had been received from 15 percent of all customers who had purchased the HPPI8-A and further shipments of the product had been halted. The employees were talking and it was just a matter of time before the media picked up the story. If this happened before the board and shareholders were informed it would be unforgivable.

Jeremy wrestled with the weight of the matter and his options.

Whichever way he looked at it the buck stopped with him. Blaming Mark for having piled pressure on him would be a pretty lame excuse. After all, he could have stood his ground against Mark, and he did not. In any case, Mark was not here to speak for himself, so Jeremy would look as if he was just trying to cover his bases by passing the buck.

Jeremy was head of production when the product was being developed. And now, he was the CEO. He just had to take responsibility. He had no idea though, how much was at stake.

The key lessons I learned in this chapter

The action steps I will take as a result

CHAPTER 7

MENTORING MOMENTS

> *Mentoring is a brain to pick, an ear to listen, and a push in the right direction.*
> John C. Crosby

A Friend In Need

Jeremy called Eric, who was now back from his vacation abroad. As soon as Eric answered the call, Jeremy fired, "Eric, I need to speak with you. It's urgent. Can you make this evening at six o'clock?" The intensity of his voice was enough to convince Eric to reorganize his schedule. He didn't receive SOS calls from his protégé every day.

Jeremy and Eric met at a private club where they were both members. On the horizon, the sun was a sinking red ball, the air was warm, and a light breeze blew the plants. The terrace was the unanimous choice for their meeting.

The atmosphere seems so…so right, I wish my life was just as orderly, Jeremy mused as he took his seat.

The two engaged in small talk about their families while they waited for their drinks. As soon as the drinks were served, Jeremy took one sip and then blurted out, "So much has happened over the past few months, it feels like a lifetime!" He briefed Eric on his first main hurdle in office revolving around Bob, the investigation, and subsequent dismissal.

Jeremy then said, "With the exit of CEO and head of sales and marketing in quick succession, I won't be surprised if I'm the next senior executive to exit!"

Eric was taken aback, "What do you mean? Sounds like you're handling your new role well, despite the headaches."

"I thought so too," Jeremy responded. "Until a few weeks ago." He then told Eric about the issue around the high precision instrument. He talked about his predicament over the way forward and concluded, "the way things have been going, it can only get worse."

The two men sipped their drinks in silence for a few minutes. Finally, Eric said, "This has been on your plate for at least a few weeks, and I suppose you've considered some options for the way forward." It sounded more of a question than a statement. Jeremy knew Eric had never been one to dish out ready-made answers. Instead, he preferred to draw them out from his mentee. For once though, Jeremy secretly wished that Eric could share his own thoughts on some possible courses of action.

Jeremy said quietly, "The only option that looks viable right now is to step down as CEO."

"What do you mean, 'step down'? Give up your position but remain as an employee of PTI Industries?"

"Oh, no, no!" Jeremy said emphatically. "Resign from the company. I need to take responsibility for what has happened."

"I'm a little confused. As you and I know, part of being a leader is taking responsibility for your actions *and* taking remedial action. Given the nature of the problem at hand, please help me understand exactly how vacating office will help solve it."

Jeremy thought for a moment. "I sincerely appreciate your helping me process this. Beyond stepping aside, I've thought about instituting a product recall and then putting in place a system to investigate and fix the glitch. If the problem is not fully resolved by the time I vacate office, I will make myself available to continue supporting the team even after I've left."

"That approach sounds workable," said Eric. "After that, what follows?"

"I haven't given much thought to it," Jeremy admitted. "To be quite honest, I love what I do at PTI Industries. My job represents so much more than just helping feed my family and pay my bills. I'm not trying to be religious, but I see it as a calling. So I can't imagine not being a part of what, over the years, has become more than an employer to me." Jeremy scratched his chin uncertainly, "For now the least I can do is take responsibility for my blunder and help to get things back on track as much as possible. Resultant costs to the company could be felt for months or even years after I am gone. I wish there was a way I could stay on and help turn things around."

Eric nodded with understanding. "When I was growing up, my favorite uncle used to talk a lot about the virtue of taking responsibility for one's mistakes and learning from them. He was a lot older, more experienced and wiser than my brother and I, so we listened to him and learnt a great deal from him. Many of those lessons have significantly contributed to making me the person I am today, and have helped me in my career too.

"Every great leader faces a major crisis at least once in their lifetime. Your actions, and not the crisis itself, is what determines whether you, as the leader, comes out a better person or worse off. The situation facing you now is a defining one. Will you allow it to make you stronger or break you? One thing you can be sure of is that you can count on my support as you weather the storm." With those words, Eric gave Jeremy a reassuring pat on the shoulder.

Jeremy smiled, "Thanks, Eric. Your support means a great deal to me."

Over the next hour, the two men talked about how Jeremy could break the news to the board chair, and probable career moves for Jeremy.

The News

That night, Jeremy telephoned Madame P. *These night calls are becoming frequent,* he thought. After apologizing for the late call, he said he urgently needed to meet with her the following day. The only slot she had was lunch time, so they agreed to meet over a quick meal.

Despite his conversation with Eric having ended on a positive note, the night turned out to be one of the longest ever. Jeremy's wife Tanya, with whom he had been talking throughout the period of the investigation, tried to reassure him that all would be well. Though well meant, her words sounded empty to Jeremy. *What does she know about PTI Industries and its current priorities?* He pondered. The top agenda for the board and shareholders was to see the company turned around to profitability. Any distracting sideshows would be neither tolerated nor accommodated.

Jeremy was in the office early the next day. Over the next few hours, he ran through his prepared script over and over again.

Finally, as the time for his meeting with Madame P drew closer, he left for the restaurant where they were to meet. She arrived five minutes after him.

Already indicating that she would be rushing to another engagement after their appointment, they placed their orders promptly. As they took their drinks while waiting for the food, Jeremy took a deep breath. "I'm not sure where to begin but I need to tell you about the high precision instruments project."

Madame P listened intently without interrupting. Her face had turned serious. "Three days ago I got a call from one of the board members," she began. "He had received a call from a member of your executive team hinting about the same issue. He didn't have factual information, though, so we agreed that he find out more before I call you. I didn't want to act on a rumor that could have turned out unfounded. I appreciate your sharing this information with me."

Jeremy didn't know whether to be relieved or annoyed. *Who on the executive team could have made the call?* He wondered. Almost immediately he held himself in check. *What does it matter? The news would have got out anyway. I should be grateful that Madam P had the good sense not to blow up immediately.*

He was jolted back to the conversation by Madam P's question, "What steps have you taken to resolve the matter?"

Jeremy was quick to respond. "The full report only came in yesterday, so no action yet. However, I have some initial thoughts which I'll be discussing with the heads of production, sales and marketing, and corporate communications this afternoon. They include a recall of all units shipped, a press release to stem damaging media coverage and criticism, correction of the fault and, of course, intensive customer service for our existing and potential clients."

Madam P said, "I'm glad you already have ideas covering various bases. How about any impact on staff jobs and competitor reactions?"

"Impact on staff will become clear once we determine the extent of the damage" said Jeremy. "That's because only then will we know the corrective action required and who will be involved. Nevertheless, we'll do our best to minimize job losses both in production and sales. The saving grace with our rivals is that there is still no direct competition for the affected product. Two of our closest contenders have been trying to import a comparable item, but the process has been slow because of government legislation which needs to be amended to accommodate the imports. Regardless, any delay on our part in correcting the problem will give the competitors mileage to lobby with the government over the pending legislation. We need to move with speed so as not to lose our solid footing in the market."

"I'm glad there are concrete plans to sort out the mess." Madam P said. "We will of course need to discuss your role in the whole matter. We cannot underplay the seriousness of this, so the board and shareholders will have to be brought into the picture right away. I will call a special board meeting as soon as possible to deliberate on the way forward."

Lunch was served and as they started eating, Jeremy said pensively, "I've considered my role to some degree. I take full responsibility for what has happened, and therefore will be tendering my resignation by the date of the board meeting. I will avail myself for as long as I'm needed to help clean up the mess and ensure a smooth transition."

Madam P neither protested nor accepted Jeremy's suggestion. "I will let the shareholders and board members know your thoughts. Let's leave the matter till then. For now, I would appreciate regular updates on the situation which I will be sharing with the board."

They discussed routine company matters over their lunch, and agreed to touch base on phone within two days. As they parted ways at the parking, Jeremy wondered what the future held for him. For the time being though, he had plenty of work cleaning up the mess and there was the board meeting to think about.

Special Meeting

Before the special board meeting, Madam P held a conference call with the company's five shareholders and briefed them on what had happened. Four of them reacted explosively. They strongly argued for the acceptance of Jeremy's offer to resign, effective immediately. The fifth and majority shareholder wasn't convinced that was the way to go. "Let's look at the matter objectively instead of just reacting," he appealed. "Profits are down, and now there's this mess. While Jeremy has a part to play, he's not the only problem on our hands. Sacking him will only be a partial solution to the problem. We need to take a much longer-term view. What will be gained from releasing him? What could be lost? How will the action affect the rest of the staff?"

After a fair amount of back and forth, they acknowledged that the board had a better grip on the company's delicate situation and other constraints that could possibly affect the workability of any decision they would make. In the end, they decided to give the board the power to carefully evaluate the options and decide on the matter.

What would tip the balance, and in what direction?

Board Meeting

When the board members arrived for the special meeting, most had sober looks on their faces. Madam P had already briefed them on the subject of the unusual gathering and they braced themselves for the discussion ahead.

Madam P opened the meeting, read out the agenda, and invited Jeremy to give the detailed report.

Jeremy sounded strangely calm as he narrated in great detail the origin of the problem, talked about the steps already taken to address it, and concluded with further proposed action steps. When he was done, one member wanted to know, "Did you say Mark pressurized you into moving to production prematurely?"

Jeremy was careful to clear any misunderstanding, "Mark was concerned about the long delay before the product's release. As the person with technical expertise in that situation, I should have advised him about the importance of waiting till after the final test. I did not."

"O, I see," the member sounded satisfied.

There were no more questions, therefore Madam P requested Jeremy to excuse members of the board so they could talk about the matter.

As soon as Jeremy stepped out, Chris, an outspoken member, said, "Let's start with the easier part."

Marilyn, who had been on the board for less than a year joined in quickly, "What do you consider the easier part?"

Chris had a ready answer. "The proposed steps to clear the mess. What to do about Jeremy will be a hard tackle." There was unanimous agreement with Chris' proposed approach.

The board members first considered and approved the press release, product recall and corrective action to fix the fault in HPPI8-A. They also consented to extensive customer service. The company, they decided, would cover shipping costs related to all returns of defective items. They would need to look for ways to cut down costs and delay any expenditure which would not jeopardize critical operations.

A long-drawn-out discussion ensued around what disciplinary action to take against Jeremy. They went back and forth between letting him go and giving him another chance. Majority of the board members were concerned about lack of a strong alternative internal candidate, as had become evident during the recent CEO recruitment exercise. The idea of an external search was floated. This was instantly ruled out, considering the fact that the process would likely take more time than the company could currently afford to lose. In under six months, the company had seen Mark and Bob leave. Jeremy would be the third senior figure to go. And if he was replaced by a CEO who was from outside the company, the board was concerned that the company's top leadership would be significantly weakened. The new CEO would start off without strong support, and would therefore be in a highly vulnerable position. Literally a set up for failure.

As if that was not bad enough, sacking Jeremy at this time would only deal staff morale another blow that could lead to further staff losses. And that would have a negative spillover effect on sales and customer service. It would be downhill all the way. Whichever way they looked at it, there would be too much at risk in firing Jeremy.

Although retaining Jeremy was no guarantee that things would change for the better, the board was willing to take a gamble on him. They decided that it was in the company's best interests to retain him, if only to help stabilize the company and buy time as they looked for another CEO. They would however put conditions around his remaining in office.

Before then, his appointment as CEO had not been subject to any probation period given the number of years he had previously been with the company. The board now regretted this fact. Henceforth, he would be put on a one-year probation and be required to check in with the board chair before making any major decisions, strategic or operational, during this time.

Another omission was not having given Jeremy clearly spelled out performance targets. Erroneously, it was assumed that he would automatically succeed in turning around the company's performance. How reckless they had been! In a quick timespan, the board had been proved wrong-twice. They had no choice but to keep close watch going forward.

They called Jeremy back into the meeting.

Walking nervously into the room, Jeremy scanned the board members' faces to try and get an indication of what had transpired in his absence. Nothing! No hint whatsoever about the decision they had made. *Whatever will be, will be,* Jeremy thought, resignedly.

Sliding into this seat, he clasped his hands under the table and steeled himself to hear the worst. In her characteristic composed manner, Madam P said, "The board has decided to retain you in your position."

"What?" Jeremy almost shouted. "You're saying that I should continue in the CEO role?"

Madam P nodded, "That's correct. However, we saw it fit to add some special conditions to your contract which we expect you to adhere to…" The rest of her statement was lost to Jeremy as he drifted between elation at what he had just heard, and disbelief. He thought he might wake up to find that he had only been dreaming.

He was grateful when Madam P addressed him by name, which caught his attention, "Jeremy, your revised terms of service will include a one-year probation period and rigorous performance targets which we'll be reviewing monthly. We will work with HR to get you the revised contract before the end of the week." She didn't ask Jeremy whether the terms were agreeable to him.

Under normal circumstances, the presumption that I'll accept the terms without question would bother me, Jeremy thought. *Not now. You don't get a lifeline thrown at you every day.*

That literally marked the beginning of a new chapter for Jeremy.

He rubbed his hands together, took a long, deep breath and said, "Thank you for giving me another chance. I promise…" Madam P cut him short, "Don't make any hasty promises you could regret later."

Jeremy let whatever he was going to say pass.

Madam P wished him all the best and dismissed the meeting.

One after the other, the members shook hands with Jeremy and left.

The key lessons I learned in this chapter

The action steps I will take as a result

CHAPTER 8

NEW CHAPTER?

New beginnings are often disguised as painful endings.
Lao Tzu

Together We Can

On the way back to his office, Jeremy stopped by his personal assistant's desk. Enid was lost in a report she was working on, but looked up as he approached.

"Enid, please call the executive team members and ask them to meet me in the boardroom in half an hour. It's urgent."

Walking into his office, he closed the door behind him and punched the air with his fist. He got on the phone immediately. "Guess what Tanya?" He told his wife excitedly. "It's a new beginning for me! The board has decided to let me stay on. Can you believe it? They've put in a few conditions, of course, but compared to what I was expecting, it feels like just a slap on the wrist."

Tanya, who knew how much this meant to Jeremy, cried, "Woo-hoo! I'm doing the happy dance for you!"

Jeremy was grateful for his wife's support. "Thank you! Your confidence and support mean a lot to me. I need to make another quick call and chair a brief meeting, so I need to go now. I just wanted you to be the first one to know the good news. See you later!"

Next, he called Eric. Trying to sound serious, he said, "Want to guess what happened?" Eric laughed, "Your voice is a complete give away! Don't tell me you no longer need my assistance to pack and move office. How disappointing!"

They both laughed heartily at the joke, before Jeremy cut in, "I don't know the details of why they decided to retain me and maybe it is best that I don't for now. What I do know is that they were gracious enough to give me a second chance. I owe it to myself, to the board, the staff, and to the company to do everything within my power to make sure I won't need a third chance."

There was a knock on Jeremy's door. Enid stepped in, gave the thumbs up sign and left. "Eric, I have to go now, but I look forward to catching up when we have more time to talk."

Eric, equally jubilant at the turn of events said, "Sure, buddy. You know I've got your back. Always!"

Jeremy buzzed Enid. "All set?" he enquired.

"Apart from Jake Bima who's away on leave, and Nancy Bobo who's in a meeting out of the office, everyone else confirmed." Enid beamed.

"Great, thanks," said Jeremy. He hung up, reached in his top drawer and took out a spiral-bound ruled book that he jokingly referred to as his thinking partner. Its brown leather cover was worn out with use. Opening a fresh page, he started scribbling quickly. He needed to organize his thoughts around what he was going to share with his team shortly. For another fifteen minutes he alternated between scribbling, pausing, and flipping through his book. Finally, he put it back in the drawer and made his way to the boardroom.

Eleanor Meja, acting head of sales and marketing since Bob's departure, was a few steps ahead of him. Olivia Lima, head of strategy, and Maureen were already in the room. Eleanor took the seat next to Olivia. Just then, Shirley of HR, and Ryan from corporate communications, came in laughing. Only Helen of legal was missing. She hurriedly walked in as Jeremy kicked off the meeting.

"Good afternoon, ladies and gentlemen. Please accept my deepest appreciation for your making the time to attend this meeting at such short notice. To honor your time, I won't keep you long." He cleared his throat, and then continued. "Most of what I have to say is not new to Eleanor, Ryan and Maureen. We have a problem on our hands, and regrettably, I'm responsible"

Eleanor nodded, while Ryan and Maureen exchanged quick glances. The rest didn't seem overly surprised, which implied they had some information on the matter. Knowing how important it was to set things out formally and clear any misinformation, he went on. "We have a glitch in the new product, HPPI8-A, which has negative repercussions."

Jeremy summarized how the problem had come up, what led to its discovery and the actions in place. He said that the executive team would be updated on the matter on a regular basis and then he invited questions.

"What are the financial implications, both current and future?" Shirley wanted to know.

Jeremy decided to play it safe and responded simply, "We are still assessing the damage; but are also doing everything we can to stem further losses." He knew it sounded fuzzy, but decided that fueling the situation unnecessarily was the least helpful thing to do at this time. Fortunately, Shirley did not press further.

He asked them to relay the same information to their teams, and concluded the meeting on a positive note. "I am confident that together we will turn this great company around and subsequently put it on the path of sustainable growth and margins."

Remedy

A press release was sent out immediately outlining the discovery of the defect, remedial action to be taken and assuring prospective clients that appropriate steps would be taken to mitigate against future recurrence of the same.

Within days, clients who had purchased the instrument were contacted and presented with replacements of the defective parts at no extra cost. The company also offered to cover shipping costs both ways. It took several weeks to replace defective parts as some of the clients took longer than expected to ship back what they had purchased.

Deeper In The Red

Jeremy's buoyancy at being thrown the proverbial lifeline was short-lived. In the midst of mopping up the mess after the HPPI8-A recall, the CFO, Nancy, came to see him. She had two copies of summary financial reports, and she handed one to Jeremy. It took Jeremy only a couple of minutes to skim through and realize that the company's financial results for the second quarter ever since he took over as CEO were grim. Whereas the first quarter results had been bad, the second quarter results could only be termed as catastrophic.

He moaned. "Oh no! I knew the faulty part was going to cost us heavily, but this is disastrous! Facing the board over this is the last thing that I want to do..." he trailed off. He didn't have any energy left to fight, and calmly said, "Please take me through the report."

As Nancy reviewed the report in detail, the gravity of the situation became clearer. Over the last week alone, PTI Industries was not only deeper in the red, it was now having liquidity problems. Reportedly, in the last three days several creditors who called for payment had been turned away, and a few had threatened legal action. The company's net worth had dropped further in the last three months from an already negative position.

Jeremy sighed audibly as he thought, *feels like I've hit rock bottom and there's nowhere else to go in deeper.*

Board Meeting

Jeremy's stomach was in knots as he presented the financial reports at the next board meeting. After some discussion on the results, he was asked to step outside for the board to caucus. *I'm getting used to this routine now,* he thought wryly, as he stepped out of the boardroom.

Heading back to his office, he closed the door behind him and went straight to his desk. He opened the top drawer and pulled out his thinking companion. He flipped through it slowly, pausing every now and then to scribble something in the margins. About halfway through, he stopped suddenly as if something had just dawned on him. He closed the journal abruptly and then put it carefully on the left hand side of his desk. He walked over to the bookshelf. Scanning the rows of books, he picked five copies which were from his home library. He put them on top of his thinking companion. He then picked the two family pictures sitting on top of the bookshelf and put them on the growing pile on his desk.

He walked to the wall farthest from his desk and picked the lone painting. Dislodging it from its place on the wall, he held it gingerly and turned it over a couple of times. It was a painting of a group of marathoners, each with a look of determination on his face. Tanya had painstakingly painted it over a three-week period soon after he shared with her his personal philosophy of leadership being like a marathon. He treasured it. It had pride of place in each office he occupied since then.

Carrying it back to his desk, he placed it next to the books and photos. Just then, his telephone rang. It was Madam P, inviting him back to the board room.

I'm not surprised they didn't need too much time this time round, he mused on the way back to the boardroom.

Madam P was brief. "Jeremy, you and your team have a lot to do over the coming months. Top on the list will be engaging an outside firm to carry out an employee engagement survey."

What Madam P was saying didn't make sense at all to Jeremy. He had left the board discussing the company's financial performance and back in his office, he had started packing in readiness for his immediate exit from PTI Industries. Now Madam P was talking about an employee assessment involving him and his team.

Jeremy didn't know whether to be relieved or confused. *What did I miss? Even more importantly, what is the board up to? Are they laying a trap for me? There seems to be no end to the drama!*

Picture Falling Into Place

Fortunately, Jeremy didn't have to wonder for long. Madam P formally closed the board meeting and as the rest of the members filed out, she and Marilyn stayed behind.

"I'm sure you're wondering what's going on?" Madam P asked.

Jeremy, still in a daze from the unexpected turn of events, nodded but didn't say anything.

"Several weeks ago, Marilyn shared with me a journal article about employee engagement and its impact on business outcomes," said Madame P. "She quoted various research studies which have concluded that employee engagement drives business results. Marilyn suggested that the board consider initiating an employee engagement survey for the company. As you no doubt know, the survey provides a comprehensive view of the organization from the inside. You possibly know of Gallup, an organization that has carried out extensive research in the area. They define engaged employees as those who are involved in, enthusiastic about, and committed to their work and workplace."

Madam P looked at Marilyn who nodded in agreement but did not interrupt. "Marilyn has worked for two companies that carried out similar surveys and reportedly changed their fortunes for the better, so she was insistent about the need for such an exercise here. To further drive her point home, she included her own personal observations about her initial impressions of PTI Industries when she first joined the board. She highlighted declining performance, apparent apathy among a significant section of the staff, high turnover, and leadership challenges. According to Marilyn, all these were symptomatic of a deeper issue pointing to a lack of employee engagement.

I decided to share the article from Marilyn and her thoughts with the non-executive board members.

"What followed was an intense discussion about the potential benefits of carrying out a staff engagement survey at this time. Board members were split half between carrying out a survey or not. In the end we decided to revisit the matter in six months' time and see whether views will have changed."

Madam P's voice changed. She sounded emphatic, "When we saw the financial report you sent ahead of today's meeting, we knew we had to do something different. After a fair amount of back and forth discussions, carrying out a staff engagement survey became the unanimous next step. We want employees to feel listened to which will help unearth underlying issues that are sabotaging performance. Consequently, the survey results will form the basis of an action plan to address the challenges once and for all. But we needed to formalize the discussion in a structured meeting. Now you know why we called you back into the meeting so quickly."

It all made perfect sense to Jeremy.

Madame P shot a warning. "Unfortunately for you, we're not giving you a choice on this one. We expect you to draw some ideas from Marilyn's experience in moving things forward. I'll leave you to discuss finer details with her now so you can get it done without any delays. Let's do a review in a month's time.

Call me if you have any questions." With that, she stretched out her hand to Jeremy, shook his and left.

Marilyn was the first to speak. "Working with an outside firm ensures objectivity in the whole process. They will run the engagement survey, help interpret results and benchmark engagement levels against other organizations of our nature and size. I have a reliable contact that you could work with."

She got out her cellphone, scrolled down her address book, found the number she was looking for and sent it to Jeremy. "That's the number for Natalie of Engage Associates. I've worked with her before so please tell her that I referred you. I can vouch for her professionalism and ability to help companies get to the bottom of underlying issues, and then move on to improve productivity and results. I'm more than happy to sit in your first meeting with her."

"Great!" Jeremy said. "I'll call her right away, so we can agree on a day and time that works for all of us." He called Natalie. After a brief introduction, he explained why he was calling and secured an appointment for later in the week. He and Marilyn chatted for a few more minutes, and then she left.

Jeremy walked slowly back to his office. Seeing the pile of items sitting neatly on his desk, he rubbed his eyes and shook his head unbelievably. "Unimaginable wonders!" He said aloud.

He hung the prized painting on the wall, picked up the books and family photos and placed them back on the bookshelf, and then he put his thinking companion back in the drawer.

Picking his blazer and car keys, he made his way out. He only stopped briefly by Enid's desk to say he was having an early evening.

Turning Point

The next day, Jeremy briefed Shirley of HR on the board meeting and ensuing decision. Two days later, he, Shirley and Marilyn held the introductory meeting with Natalie. Over the next week, terms of engagement were negotiated and firmed up, and the survey conducted shortly thereafter.

By the time Jeremy met with Madam P for a review one month later, Natalie had a draft report from the survey. "As you already know, PTI Industries has experienced significant leadership transitions, employee turnover has been high and morale low. That's as bad as declining companies get. The good news is that all this can be turned around." That seemed to be the cue the three were waiting for, as they leaned in almost simultaneously.

"Among the key recommendations are: ensure that every member of the executive team gets into a formal coaching relationship with a professional coach; train everyone else who manages people; and develop on-going staff development programs for employees at all levels. Contrary to popular but misguided and misinformed beliefs, staff training and development is a necessity for any forward-looking organization working towards sustainably improving results. It is not an optional operating expense."

No one questioned the recommendations. Instead, they agreed that implementation should start right away.

Starting the week after, Natalie worked with Shirley and Jeremy to design a coaching program for the executive team members. Input was sought from the team, to ensure buy-in and ownership right from the start. Another month, and the program was firmly in place.

Jeremy was frenetically busy in the weeks that followed. In between discussing strategic interventions with his executive team or engaging the board and employees on one matter or the other, he had regular coaching and mentoring sessions with Eric and the company-hired coach.

Eric continued to share valuable leadership lessons drawn from his experience in running his own businesses. Jeremy liked the fact that they were transferable lessons which he could easily relate to, as a CEO. They centered around leading self, building relationships, balancing personal and professional matters, and generating results through others. And from his work with the other coach, he drew valuable lessons on handling challenges and failure, and allowing those experiences to shape him into a better person and leader.

With all the learning and meaningful engagement all round, he slowly settled down into a new routine. Crazy as his schedule was, he found himself looking forward to each new day and its challenges. A quiet confidence that he had not experienced before grew inside him, giving him a lot of hope that he would pull through successfully. He resolved to give the new window of opportunity his best.

Surprise Visitor

Out of the blue late one morning, Enid called to say that Jeremy had an important visitor. She declined to give details. Jeremy trusted her judgment and agreed to see the mystery visitor.

He was totally unprepared to see Mark stride confidently into his office. He couldn't help exclaiming, "What brings you here?" He quickly added, "Please don't get me wrong. It's not that I don't want to see you, I just never imagined…" his voice trailed off. He was unsure what to make of the visit considering their difficult relationship previously. "Jeremy, you don't need to explain. I would possibly react in the same way if I was in your shoes," Mark said, giving Jeremy a hearty handshake. He then apologized for dropping by without appointment, but explained that he had been feeling a strong urge to come and see him.

Jeremy welcomed Mark to sit, "Please tell me how you've been, and how Alison is doing."

Mark didn't need persuading. He talked about his wife's treatment program, great lessons he had learned as he stood by her during that period, moments of reflection and more. Jeremy found himself totally drawn to Mark's stories. He had to admit that the Mark in his office looked and sounded very much unlike the man he had interacted with before. He was refreshingly pensive and mellow.

That made Jeremy feel comfortable enough to spontaneously talk about his own experiences since Mark's departure. He concluded, "The best part of it all is that I've been able to focus on the positive side of the tough moments I've gone through. I'm wiser and stronger as a result." Mark nodded in understanding and said, "Hang in there and weather the storms. They will pass."

Mark finally surprised Jeremy by saying, "I wish I had listened when you invited me to lunch and offered to support me in addressing leadership gaps at the company. At the time, I thought you were challenging my leadership but I've since come to appreciate the role even presumably less experienced leaders can play in the lives of more senior and experienced leaders." Jeremy responded graciously, "No hard feelings, Mark. The most important thing is that the past isn't holding either of us back. We are here to learn from one another."

Mark stood up, "I need to run along so you also proceed with your work. Why don't we get together for a drink, sometime?"

"Sounds good," said Jeremy as he shook Mark's hand. "Let's do it." As Jeremy watched Mark leave, he felt as if a heavy load had been lifted from his shoulders. It dawned on him that he had unconsciously lived under the cloud of a previously strained relationship quite unnecessarily. It was as if Mark's visit had magically instilled in him renewed focus and energy.

He resolved to put his whole heart and mind to re-scripting his story at PTI Industries.

A New Dawn

Jeremy's new air of enthusiasm was palpable. What was more, it became contagious and started catching on to the rest of the staff. Employees regularly stopped him along the corridors to share ideas for improvement. Conversations around the coffee machine were noticeably more about issues and exchange of information, and less about differences and personalities.

Three months later, financial results showed a slight improvement, though the company was still suffering effects of the HPPI8-A recall and did not break even. But that improvement proved to be another spark that reignited enthusiastic effort amongst staff across the board.

Another three months down the line, PTI Industries broke even financially. Given results for the first three quarters however, the overall results for the year were disappointing. Nonetheless that did not stop Jeremy from leading the executive team in applauding staff for their improved performance and contribution to the company. Even the board agreed that the positive trend was encouraging.

There was still another six months before Jeremy's probation was due for review. By the time the review came round, results for another two quarters were in. They were consistently stronger and the turnaround had been nothing short of a miracle. When Jeremy received news that plans for a new CEO search had been abandoned, he was immensely relieved.

Leaders Don't Cross the Finish Line Alone

Jeremy was elated by the continued improved results. In his moment of success and renewed confidence, he remembered the wise words of one of his favorite authors: 'Leaders don't cross the finish line alone'.

He acknowledged the fact that the ongoing success had not been due to his efforts alone and gave credit to all who had contributed to the company's upward trend. He was extremely grateful that the board had given him extra chances when he didn't deserve them, the space to perform, and that they remained supportive. He was grateful that the executive team had worked closely together, and that staff had given ideas and feedback and thrown their weight solidly behind him.

Even more importantly, his mentor and coach had believed in him. He remembered how on some days he had felt ready to throw in the towel. But the support granted along the way and his personal conviction that things would eventually work out kept him going.

Had it been worth it? Every bit!

Unsurprisingly, things were going well in his private life too. He continued to enjoy Tanya's support and occasionally found himself smiling at her picture as he sat in his office. On one such days, he found himself thinking, *it's not just leadership which is a marathon. Marriage is a marathon. Parenting is a marathon. Life is one big marathon. There are days I've felt totally drained and ready to throw in the proverbial towel, but I see now how much I would have lost in the process. Whatever it takes, I'll keep moving. My eyes are on the finish line and I'll get there!*

The key lessons I learned in this chapter

The action steps I will take as a result

CHAPTER 9

YEARNING FOR MORE

We rise by lifting others.
Robert Ingersoll

Odd

It was ironical that something rather odd began to happen. Barely six months after his confirmation into office by the board, Jeremy found himself getting lethargic. He was strangely feeling restless about the success he was now enjoying and secretly wondered whether that signaled a desire for a job change. Was it time for a new challenge? While this notion seemed unlikely as he did not have a habit of constantly changing jobs, he couldn't quite shake it off. So he allowed it to simmer in the background.

A few months later, he received a call from Peter Kabo, an old classmate and friend.

After graduating from university, Peter had worked for a multinational company for several years and risen through the ranks in HR. He later left to set up his own consulting and recruitment firm. Now in its tenth year, Peter's outfit was a key player in the industry.

Though the two had kept close tabs on one another after university, they had not connected in a couple of years. Jeremy wondered why Peter might be calling him now. He didn't have to wonder for long.

"Jeremy, guess what I have for you?" Peter beamed.

Jeremy was not in the mood for guessing games, "Spill the beans, will you?" he shot back.

His response did not dampen Peter's enthusiasm, who said, "One of my A-list clients is looking for a group CEO. They are a leading player in their industry, which presents a good challenge and excellent growth prospects for the position. The pay and perks are great, and include a share ownership plan. You fit the candidate profile perfectly!"

Jeremy was flattered, "Thanks, buddy! Let me think about it and get back to you."

"No problem," Peter said. "You won't regret the move!"

Jeremy felt a tinge of excitement at the prospect of a new and bigger challenge coupled with the promise of handsome rewards. Strangely though, the excitement didn't last long. A week later, he called Peter and thanked him for the consideration, but quickly added that he wouldn't pursue the opportunity.

Peter was stunned, "Hey, mate, what's up with you? The job is a perfect match, and the reward package is great!" He tried pressuring Jeremy to reconsider his decision, even offering to give him more time to think through it.

Jeremy was firm. No, he wasn't interested. Silently, he was as relieved as he was surprised at himself. That he could walk away from such an offer and still feel a reassuring peace about having made the right decision was something he neither understood, nor could explain.

Light-bulb Moment

Exactly a month later, an incident with his team became a light-bulb moment to Jeremy. The executive team was having a half-day off-site meeting to review plans for an upcoming, high-profile project.

An informal discussion among the group during tea break turned to staff matters. Mainly there were encouraging stories about employees continuing to take initiative to come up with innovative solutions to business problems, and about selfless acts of thoughtfulness and team spirit among staff. This went on for a while until the CIO, Jake, spoke up. He said that while everyone else on his team was pulling their weight, there was an exception.

His information systems manager was a young man named Marcus. Marcus had been with PTI Industries for seven months, was highly intelligent and hard working. His input was key to the overall success of the team. Nonetheless, he had proved a pain to work with because of what Jake referred to simply as a 'rotten attitude'. He withheld critical information from others and went to great lengths to shine as an individual at the expense of his team members. Jake had warned him several times but since he hadn't improved, he was now seriously thinking of letting him go.

For some reason, Jeremy found himself taking interest in Marcus. He wondered whether it had to do with his own experience, having been fired from his first job and someone reaching out to him. He wished he could help Marcus make the most of the opportunity he had at PTI Industries and not waste his chances.

But he wanted to mull over it first before making a promise he couldn't follow through, so he didn't say anything to Jake at the meeting. Undeniably though, there was more than just a casual interest in pursuing the matter.

Paying It Forward

The week after the off-site event, Marcus was still on Jeremy's mind and the conviction to help was even stronger. He rang Jake.

"When we had the off-site meeting, you talked about a young man on your team who's been difficult to work with. How are things with him now?" asked Jeremy.

"Marcus? He's worse. I've given him more than enough warnings, and I'll be letting him go at the end of the month," said Jake.

"Have you informed him?"

"Not yet. We have a divisional meeting on Wednesday after which I'll speak with him."

Jeremy chose his words carefully, "You know very well that I don't normally interfere with decisions that my executive team members make. However, I beg your indulgence this once. I've found it difficult to get that young man off my mind. Whether it has to do with the rocky start to my career is a question I haven't settled yet. What I do know is that with your permission, I'd like to see whether I can help Marcus."

"What do you mean by 'help'?" Jake asked.

"I'm thinking of offering to mentor and coach him. It will all depend, of course, on whether Marcus is open to being helped. As the saying goes, you can take a camel to the river but you cannot force it to drink. You can though, give the camel a little salt to make it thirsty. I can have a chat with Marcus to try and help him see what's at stake and how he stands to benefit if he throws his weight behind the team. It will be my way of putting salt on his tongue. Beyond that, it's his call."

Jake chuckled at the analogy, but then quickly got serious. "You could be wasting your time." It was now his turn to choose his words carefully. "Marcus doesn't seem interested in changing. But if it makes you feel better, you have my blessing."

"My friend and mentor, Eric, likes to say that no one is beyond repair. I'd like to see what I can do. Please ask Marcus to see me in my office tomorrow at 11:30 a.m." With that, Jeremy put his receiver down.

Jake's words that he was possibly wasting his time rang in his mind for a minute or two. But the conviction that he couldn't write Marcus off without at least trying to help him was stronger. In any case, what was the worst that could happen? If Marcus was not interested in changing, he would be let go of, making room for someone else—perhaps more teachable—to join the team. Jeremy would have no regrets for having tried to help. It would be Marcus' loss.

The Meeting

As Jeremy waited to meet with Marcus at 11:30 a.m. the following day, he reviewed a keynote speech he would be delivering at an industry group dinner later in the week. The general thrust of his message was about more seasoned professionals needing to invest in younger, less experienced workers. He briefly relieved the previous day's conversation with Jake. *Yes, I am not going to preach water and drink wine!* One investment in a talented employee who needed it was worth it.

At 11:35 am there was no sign of Marcus.

At 11:40 am, Jeremy wondered whether to call Jake to find out if he had told Marcus about their proposed meeting, and then decided against it.

At 11:45a.m., his office door opened without warning. A young man, possibly in his mid-twenties, poked his face in. He was tall, a little lean and well groomed. Jeremy knew the face well, but couldn't recall having talked with him beyond a casual greeting.

"Mr. Sani? My boss, Jake said that you wanted to see me." He said in a gruff voice.

Jeremy noted, but decided not to point out, Marcus' lack of an apology for his lateness and his coming in without knocking. He would have time for that later.

"Yes, and you must be Marcus." It was more of a statement than a question. "Have a seat. And, please call me Jeremy."

Even as Marcus sat down, Jeremy noticed that he looked rather uneasy. "How is your morning, Marcus?" he enquired.

"So-so. I mean, a little better than your usual morning, but not by much."

"What would you say is a usual morning for you?" Jeremy pressed.

Marcus said casually, "I like it when I'm left to concentrate on my work. That doesn't happen often around here though, as there are numerous interruptions on most days—too many meetings and colleagues asking for assistance."

"You sound somewhat discontent." Jeremy let the sentence hang in the air.

"On the contrary, I do enjoy my work. It's the people who bother me." Marcus stopped abruptly, and looked at Jeremy as if he had said too much.

Jeremy picked up the cue gently. "How do they bother you? Don't you enjoy working with them?"

Marcus looked at Jeremy as if trying to decide whether this was a trick question. Seeming to weigh his words a little, he said, "If I get my work done, I shouldn't be held responsible for others who are working under me. As far as I'm concerned, every person takes responsibility for their own performance." It sounded more of a question than a plain statement.

Jeremy decided to delay his response and gather more information first.

"Oh, I see. I'll be the last person to tell you that there's a simple answer to your query. But it's all related to the reason for my inviting you to see me. Did Jake tell you why I asked to meet you?" Jeremy enquired. Marcus shook his head and shrugged his shoulders, but didn't say anything.

"Jake told me he has concerns about the way you relate to your colleagues, but I firmly believe there are two sides to each story. I'd like to hear yours."

Marcus shifted uneasily in his seat. He seemed to be wondering whether he had been set up.

Jeremy sought to reassure him. "Look, Marcus, I know you're wondering why I'm bothered. It's a long story that goes back many years to my first job. I made some terrible mistakes and had no one to guide me, so I got fired from that job."

Marcus sat up straight, "You? You were sacked?" It was as if talking to Jeremy was now important.

"Yes, I was sacked in what I believed was the most callous manner. Looking back now, I can say with all honesty that I deserved it. I have learned a lot since those early days, thanks largely to a friend who decided to invest in me. He mentored and coached me for many years. Sadly, he's deceased. By the time he died, however, another mentor had come along. Our relationship continues to this day, and I owe much of my success to his guidance and support.

"I now feel that I need to be passing on that which has been freely passed to me. I owe it to those younger than me, to help them avoid some of the mistakes I made and also let them learn from my successes. But of course, everyone has a choice and so I can only offer my assistance, which I know will sometimes be accepted and other times declined."

Marcus sank back in his seat and said guardedly, "I don't get the connection between what you've just said and my being here."

Jeremy realized it was going to take a lot more to win Marcus' trust. He decided to be direct.

"Look, Marcus. I don't know what is brewing in your department, but from what I've heard, things don't sound rosy. I have enough on my hands. It's not in my position to interfere with what I know could be easily handled by your departmental head and HR. From the sound of things, however, that may not necessarily work in your favor. Part of what seems to be going on resonates with me, so I decided to invite you for a chat and find out if there's any assistance I could offer. I'm thinking of an informal mentoring and coaching role with you. You don't have to take my offer, of course. It's your choice. I'd hate to see you waste the opportunity you have at PTI Industries, though.

"Tell me, what's going on?" Jeremy pressed.

Marcus shifted uncomfortably in his seat, but remained silent. Jeremy realized that his approach was not working. He had said enough for the initial meeting.

"Marcus, why don't you mull over my offer and let me know what you think tomorrow? Same time, same place?" suggested Jeremy.

There was a look of relief on Marcus' face, like a deer escaping from a snare, Jeremy thought. He smiled to himself, almost sadly, *if only he knew that my only motive is to help him.*

"Okay, sir – I mean, Jeremy," said Marcus. He quickly rose to his feet and made for the door.

An idea crossed Jeremy's mind. "Just one more thing, Marcus. My wife and I, together with a few friends, are going to watch the visiting orchestra this evening. I don't know whether you're a fan of those types of concerts but even if you're not, I can assure you that this one will be worth watching. I have an extra ticket, and wondered whether you'd be interested in joining us? Let me know by four o'clock this afternoon. If you're able to come along and need a ride, I can organize one for you. Here's my personal number." He fished out a business card, scribbled his personal cellphone number at the back and handed the card to Marcus.

"Thank you, sir – Jeremy!" Marcus said quickly and was gone.

The Show

At 3:55p.m. that afternoon, Jeremy's phone rang.

"Sir? This is Marcus. Thank you for the invitation to the concert. I'd like to come along, and I do have a ride." Marcus' voice sounded more relaxed than it had been earlier that morning.

"Great! Then let's meet outside the Braeburn Theatre at 7:45 p.m. I'll have my cellphone on. The show starts at 8:00 pm."

That evening as Jeremy drove to the concert with his wife, he told her about his pre-occupation with Marcus, their meeting, and the invitation he'd extended to Marcus.

"What do you hope to achieve with Marcus?" Tanya wondered aloud.

Jeremy had a ready answer, "a turnaround like I personally experienced. I don't think it's too much to wish for."

"You know, honey, as I've said many times before, I truly admire your value-adding mindset. Here you are with more than enough on your plate, and now you go out of your way to invest in some one that you're not even guaranteed will come round!" Tanya beamed with admiration for her husband.

"Hearing about Marcus and then meeting him reminded me of diamond mining." Jeremy said. "You dig through tons of dirt to get to a small speck of a diamond. It requires a lot of hard work, but is worth every bit of effort. Marcus is like a diamond in the rough. If he accepts my help, I'll work with him to draw out the diamond from the dirt. It's an investment I will approach with an air of optimism."

Tanya fondly touched Jeremy's hand on the steering wheel. "Enjoy the ride, honey!"

"I certainly will, with Marcus' co-operation." Jeremy responded.

For the rest of the ride, they discussed family matters.

Arriving at 7:40 pm, Jeremy was pleasantly surprised to see that Marcus was already there. He introduced him to Tanya, and then they each grabbed a drink. By the time they were done, their friends had arrived and they all went in.

The orchestra put on a splendid performance and the evening passed quickly. Jeremy was careful not to say a word about the office to Marcus. When the concert was over, they said their goodbyes and left.

Follow Up

At exactly 11:30 a.m. the following day, there was a knock on Jeremy's door and Marcus strode in.

"Good morning, sir," he said.

"Good morning, Marcus. And it's Jeremy," Jeremy said warmly.

"Jeremy," Marcus repeated. "Thank you once again for the ticket to a truly remarkable concert. It was an evening very well spent."

"I'm glad you enjoyed it," said Jeremy, noting that Marcus looked more relaxed and sounded less guarded than the day before.

"I've thought about your offer to coach and mentor me, and I must first thank you for your kindness. I know you're busy, which makes it all the more special for me. I'm honored to accept your offer. To be honest, I was feeling rather fed up with PTI Industries and was seriously contemplating leaving. Now I have something to look forward to here."

In light of their first meeting, Jeremy was astounded at how quickly Marcus seemed to have warmed up to the idea of being assisted. It sounded almost too good to be true. But he decided that highlighting the fact would serve no useful purpose. So he simply said, "I'm so glad you've decided to take up the offer. I'm greatly looking forward to working with you. Please tell me a bit about your career, and particularly your time at PTI Industries."

"I graduated from university with a First-Class Honors degree, the top student in my class. I worked for three years at another company before joining PTI Industries. It was a step up in my career and I was looking forward to working here as a manager.

"But what happened after I was hired? I found myself doing mostly the same things I was doing at my first job. Some were even below my level as a manager. As if that wasn't bad enough, I was asked to supervise two assistants who clearly didn't know what they were doing. I've often wondered why the company doesn't hire qualified people in the first place." Marcus looked at Jeremy, who looked expressionless. He went on, "Up until yesterday, I was feeling stuck. Really stuck. I had drafted my resignation letter a month ago but held off handing it in because I didn't have another job. So my staying on was just to help pay my bills."

"Did you ever discuss your concerns with your boss or even with HR?" Jeremy enquired.

"I did. My boss's response was something vague about my needing to work at different levels so as to learn the system here. He also made reference to learning to work with others, and the need for me to empower and supervise the assistants working under me. When exactly should I train them and when will I do my work? And why should I be the one supervising them? Shouldn't everyone take responsibility for their own work?"

Jeremy realized that working with Marcus would take a lot more than he had anticipated. He needed to avoid being drawn into day-to-day management issues while helping Marcus to see that the challenge being presented to him was also an opportunity to develop as a leader. But if he could get Marcus to appreciate why he needed to develop all-round and set him on that growth journey, it would be well worth it. He spoke slowly and caringly. "It looks like there's a lot we need to work through. And results won't come overnight, so we'll need to develop a plan of action and then persistently follow through with it."

Over the next half hour, Jeremy asked Marcus to tell him more about his present job, his dreams and inspirations. He did a lot of listening. To help Marcus map out a path to get him from where he was to where he wanted to go, he needed a better understanding of him.

Marcus was not just talented; he was ambitious alright!

At the end of their meeting, Jeremy proposed that the two meet for about an hour on a weekly basis, and then after a month they could reduce the meetings to once in two weeks.

The key lessons I learned in this chapter

The action steps I will take as a result

CHAPTER 10

NEW CULTURE

You can't connect the dots looking forward; you can only connect them looking backwards.
Steve Jobs

Another Chance?

That afternoon, Jeremy gave Jake a call. "I've had a couple of meetings with Marcus. The first one was a little awkward, but I think the ice has been broken. He seems keen to learn and grow." Jake was silent, so Jeremy kept talking, "For the time being, would you reconsider your decision to let him go? I'd like to see how far I can get with him."

Jake thought for a moment then said, "You sound confident about what you're doing. I don't see that there's anything to lose. Sure, let's give it a try."

Jeremy and Marcus kept up the weekly meetings. Most of that time was spent helping Marcus clarify the steps he would need to take to get to his envisioned future. In the second month they reduced meetings to fortnightly and all the while Jeremy held Marcus accountable to follow through on action items agreed between them.

Case Study

Two months into the mentoring and coaching relationship, Jake telephoned Jeremy about Marcus. As soon as Jeremy picked the call, Jake blurted out, "What have you done to that young man? He's getting transformed right before my eyes! Granted, he still has numerous rough edges to smooth out, but his change in attitude and determination to make something of himself are evident."

Jeremy had noticed the change in Marcus yet hearing an independent confirmation—and no less than from the man who was going to fire Marcus just two months before then—was gratifying. He was modest in his response. "You know, my relationship with Marcus is a willing guide, willing follower one, as it should be. Marcus has consistently followed through on his commitments, and I'm glad the work he's putting in is paying off."

Jake replied quickly, "Marcus' work may be paying off, alright, but I dare say your role has been pivotal in turning him around.

It even got me wondering whether a similar arrangement couldn't be worked out with other staff in the organization in addition to the training programs that are being put in place."

"Your words are music to my ears," Jeremy joined, happily. "I've been mulling over challenging other executive team members to get involved in formal mentoring and coaching relationships with lower cadre staff. I'm not naïve and know some might resist it because the demand on their time will be so much more. Marcus' unfolding success story is just the sort of case study that I need to sell the idea to the team." Jeremy stopped for a moment and then asked, "Could you share Marcus' story when I introduce the idea of developing a culture of mentoring and coaching?"

"More than happy to, boss!" Jake laughed heartily and Jeremy joined in.

"Great!" Jeremy responded. "I'll be speaking with Shirley about the same so that this can be spearheaded by the learning and development team under her charge."

Moving Forward

After Jeremy got off the phone with Marcus, he sat thoughtfully for a few minutes. He was grateful that the risk he had taken in investing in Marcus was reaping dividends.

He pulled out his thinking companion from the drawer and started jotting down what, until now, had remained as a blueprint only in his head.

Mentoring and Coaching Program

- Purpose: To transform and retain talent at PTI Industries
- Scope: Organization-wide. Every executive team member to mentor and coach managers under their charge, who should in turn be challenged to coach and mentor those who report to them
- Case study: Marcus, IT Manager

He would use this outline to talk through the proposed program with Shirley. Once she was sold on the idea he would leave her to flesh out the finer details with her team.

Taking Root

Two weeks later, Jeremy sat with Shirley in his office and went over the proposed program.

Shirley was enthusiastic, "I have been thinking of putting in place a similar program, but only for the HR team!"

"I'm pleased to hear you were thinking along parallel lines," Jeremy said and then challenged her, "How can it be rolled out across the company? Come ready to share some ideas at our next executive team meeting."

When the executive team met one week later, the idea was an easier sell than Jeremy had anticipated. The team had been seeing the change in Jeremy's leadership, company results were looking good, and they themselves were feeling more empowered. The details of Marcus' case study was just the icing on the cake to prove that mentoring and coaching worked not just for the higher-ups, but also for staff at lower levels in the organization.

Three Years Later

It was the silver anniversary of PTI Industries. By now the staff mentoring and coaching program had been rolled out and firmly taken root. Business had expanded to foreign markets, the company's revenue had quadrupled, and profit margins had risen steadily.

An elaborate reception to mark the company's twenty-five years in business was hosted at a local upmarket hotel. Several dignitaries were in attendance including business executives from different sectors, government officials and representatives from the local community. In speech after speech, invited speakers paid glowing tribute to PTI Industries' leadership for the company's contribution to society in the form of employment opportunities, contribution to the government treasury through taxes, and transformational community initiatives.

The last speech of the day was delivered by the board chair, Madam P. She painted a clear picture of the company's growth from a little known enterprise to the conglomerate it now was. Drawing to a close, she made a surprise announcement, "I have been on the company's board for fifteen years, ending up as board chair. I now need to make room for new leadership to take over."

At first there was silence, then the ballroom broke out in cheers and whistles. After the noise died down, Madam P said that in the true spirit of the growth the company had experienced, it was now time to give room to a new crop of leaders who would bring a breath of fresh air to the company.

"I have done my stretch. I now pass on the baton and priceless lessons I have learned in the process."

Joyce Kaduki

The key lessons I learned in this chapter

The action steps I will take as a result

CONCLUSION

The leadership journey is like a marathon, an endurance run which is not for the fainthearted. Many start the race but not all finish it. For those who manage to go all the way, there are highs and lows along the way. The ones who keep moving as they learn and put the lessons they're picking along the way into practice eventually succeed.

What does all this mean for you as a leader? As in a marathon, it is important to determine what you want out of the race. This will inform how much practice, commitment, and effort you will put into it and ultimately, the possibility of your finishing the race. The key thing is to not give up, but to keep moving until you cross the finish line. Asking for help is not a sign of weakness but of strength. Coaching and mentoring, which are twin people-development programs, can make the process easier. As a leader, you learn how to go through the inevitable success and failure cycles. You are equipped to handle success with grace, lead through conflict, and face other leadership challenges. Ultimately, you get to the finish line successfully and not just alone, but with others to whom you passed on lessons learned along the way to.

For an organization, coaching and mentoring play a significant role in the development of leaders. They facilitate talent development and retention, development of new behaviors that drive performance and ultimately, results. All this takes time though, and therefore requires a lot of persistence and determination.

Truly, leadership is a marathon.

NOTES

Anthony Karanja. "Hyvon Ng'etich Collapses and Crawls to Finish Line in US, Gets Prize Money," Daily Nation, February 16, 2015, accessed on July 9, 2015, http://www.nation.co.ke/sports/athletics/Kenyan-marathoner-crawls-to-finish-line-US-/-/1100/2625132/-/2nwnus/-/index.html

Patrick Lencioni, "*The Five Dysfunctions of a Team*"(New York: Jossey-Bass, 2002)

Gallup, Inc. "Majority of U.S. Employees Not Engaged Despite Gains." Accessed on December 2, 2015". http://www.gallup.com/poll/181289/majority-employees-not-engaged-despite-gains-2014.aspx

www.ingramcontent.com/pod-product-compliance
Lightning Source LLC
Chambersburg PA
CBHW030740180526
45163CB00003B/867